Dawning Light

Brilliancy of God's Word

Dawning Light

Brilliancy of God's Word

by Marty Gale

First Edition
Copyright © 2025 Marty Gale
First Printing, June 2025
All rights reserved.
Paperback ISBN: 978-0-9889678-5-4
E-book ISBN: 978-0-9889678-6-1

Dawning Light, 1st ed.
Copyright © 2025 by Pastor Marty Gale
Celebration Congregation
1833 56th Avenue
Greeley, CO 80634
(970) 584-7543
CelebrationCongregation.com

All rights reserved. No part of this book may be reproduced or transmitted in any form or by any means without written permission from the author.

Unless otherwise indicated, Scripture taken from The Holy Bible, New International Version®, NIV®, copyright© 1973, 1978, 1984, 2011 by Biblica, Inc.® Used by permission. All rights reserved worldwide.

Scripture references marked KJV are from The Holy Bible, King James Version, KJV, in the public domain.

Scripture quotations taken from the New American Standard Bible®, Copyright © 1960, 1962, 1963, 1968, 1971, 1972, 1973, 1975, 1977, 1995 by The Lockman Foundation. Used by permission. (www.Lockman.org)

Cover design and interior design by Dave Arns (DaveArns.com).

Table of Contents

Acknowledgements 7

Chapter 1: No Condemnation and Paul's Thorn 9
    Justification and Sanctification 11
    Condemnation and Conviction 14
    The Accuser 15
    A Further Look at Justification 16
    More About Conviction and Sanctification 17
    Paul's Thorn 23
    The Other Side 27
    Conclusion 30

Chapter 2: The Prodigal Son 33
    The Parable of the Prodigal Son 38

Chapter 3: The Divinity of HaMashiach 107
    Is Yeshua God? 107

Chapter 4: The Davidic Covenant 133

Chapter 5: Beast 151

Chapter 6: Rebuild the Temple 175
    Biblical Support for a Third Temple 176
    The Temple and Eschatology 183
    Conclusion 185

Chapter 7: The Counterfeit 187
    Nimrod 188
    Semiramis 189
    Tammuz 190
    The Counterfeit Trinity 190
    Death of Nimrod/Tammuz 193
    God's Warning 194
    A Brief Look into Church History 198
    The Two Major Christian Holidays 199
    A Further Look into Church History 203
    High Places 207
    Jewish Roots 210
    One New Man 212
    Reformation 214

Acknowledgements

Thank you to Brenda Uribe for organizing hours of teaching material and transcribing them into manuscripts.

Thank you to Milt and Brenda Uribe for your expertise and valuable time spent editing and proofreading so I can publish this 5th book.

Thank you to HaShem, my God, for the privilege of publishing the words You give me into this book that I pray will bless those who read *Dawning Light* and hopefully give them insight into the holiness of Your word.

Chapter 1:

No Condemnation
and
Paul's Thorn

"You really think you love others? Then why aren't you out on the street preaching the gospel to those who don't know Yeshua. You are such a loser."

"You call that a sermon? Why don't you just quit now and save yourself from future embarrassment."

"You really messed up that project, didn't you? It was so bad you won't ever be asked to work on another one!"

Condemnation. We all experience it in some form whether we profess to be a Christian or not. Yet the Bible tells us in the eighth chapter of Romans that believers in Yeshua do not live under condemnation. If that is the case, why do we find the heavy chains of censure dragging us down time after time? Hope drains away and feelings of despair rise higher and higher. Desperate to live a life of freedom from condemnation, we continually fall prey to it. How does we rise above these negative experiences and live that promised life?

To best answer this question, we will consider four terms that often cause confusion: justification, sanctification, condemnation, and conviction. As we comprehend the meaning of each

9

word, we will understand how to deal with condemnation and experience new freedom in our lives.

We begin with the tetragrammaton, the four-letter name of God. It consists of the Hebrew consonants yod, hey, vov, hey, commonly transcribed into English as YHVH. The tetragrammaton is known as HaShem in Hebrew, which means The Name. No one knows the exact pronunciation of YHVH. Hebrew is written with consonants only, which means any vowel can be placed between the given letters. In Biblical times, only the priesthood knew how to pronounce The Name of God. When the last priest died after the destruction of the Temple, the correct pronunciation was lost.

YHVH is a holy God. He deeply desires an intimate relationship with man. This began when He created Adam and Eve, and the three of them shared such a relationship, but their relationship was severed after Adam and Eve sinned. The result was the separation of all mankind from God. He had a plan to restore that relationship, however, and a picture of that plan is found in The Name. In a beautiful illustration of His grace, God placed a "door" within the tetragrammaton by inserting the Hebrew letter *dalet*. All Hebrew letters have a meaning, and this letter means "door." When the *dalet* is added to the letters YHVH, it spells "Judah." This conveys a very intense message that the door to God will be through Judah. More specifically, it will be through the Lion of the tribe of Judah, Yeshua HaMashiach. "Judah" is the only Hebrew word that contains the tetragrammaton, and it holds the key (door) to an intimate relationship with God. This door within God's name has the blood of Messiah on it. All who desire to enter God's presence may enter through the door, where they will be welcomed with love and mercy. What a glorious picture of God's love! People of this world chase after many gods, but our God, *Eloheinu*, is a God of mercy, love, and tender, everlasting compassion.

You may be thinking, "Oh, Pastor! You don't know what I've done. I've said awful things and done even worse, and there's no way I can ever walk through that door." I easily identify with that statement. Sin always causes one to draw back and hide from God, just as Adam and Eve did when they sinned in the Garden of Eden. Strong feelings of unworthiness and fear of rejection are difficult to overcome. The door to God remains open, however, and He continues to invite you into His presence. Answer His invitation. Enter the door of salvation, the door through which you become righteous in God's eyes. The Father waits for you, His heart overflowing with love. "Welcome. Welcome, my beloved."

"What about the Bible verses that say I must get sin out of my life? I know if I don't get rid of such-and-such a sin I won't get into heaven!" I guarantee you've heard these words. It's a prevailing belief in the church. This will be our starting point as we take our first steps toward freedom from condemnation.

Justification and Sanctification

A local church recently hosted an out-of-town evangelist who spoke on sanctification and how to live a righteous life. He said sin must be removed from one's life, and a righteous lifestyle should be pursued. He went on to say that this lifestyle would determine whether one made it into Heaven. Consider that last statement. "A righteous lifestyle guarantees one's entrance into heaven." If that were true, heaven would be a very lonely place. I don't know anyone who can live up to that standard.

What occurred in this message frequently takes place in the church. The guest speaker placed two different doctrines into one basket and identified them as the same. First, he presented the doctrine of justification. This occurs at salvation with the cleansing blood of Yeshua. It is a one-time event. When one comes to the cross of Yeshua and by faith believes the blood of the Lamb has removed his sin, he is instantly justified and cleansed for all eternity. You may be familiar with a phrase often associated with the word justified: "Just as if I'd never sinned." One cannot become more acceptable to God than he is at that moment, no matter how many good works he accomplishes. As far as God is concerned, this person is justified and a genuine child of God. His position in Christ is affirmed and his entrance into Heaven is assured.

The second doctrine in the basket was sanctification. Rather than being a one-time event, this is a life-long process of transformation into Yeshua's image. Another word for sanctification is holiness. To be sanctified, or holy, is to become separate; to come out from the world; to live separately. God is holy because He is separate from everything else in the universe. He has called His children to be holy as He is holy (1 Peter 1:16), separate from the world. To attain holiness, there must be a continuing, progressive work of the Holy Spirit and the Word of God in us.

Understand that justification and sanctification are two separate doctrines. The evangelist said a righteous lifestyle would guarantee entry into Heaven. He spoke of the transforming process *as if it were justification*, as if sanctification could save a person. Confusing these terms has plagued many believers, and it always results in condemnation.

Justification and sanctification are addressed in many Bible passages, but it isn't always clear which term a verse refers to. If only there were a little flashing sign proclaiming, "This verse is about sanctification," or, "This one is about justification." Follow this simple rule of thumb: When a verse about living a righteous lifestyle seems to jump off the page, the Holy Spirit is speaking to you. Ask Him what He wants from you. As you continue to pray and meditate, you will find within you a desire to change. This doesn't mean you are not saved or justified. Rather, the Holy Spirit is encouraging you to work with Him. You have been invited to take part in the sanctification process.

CHAPTER 1: NO CONDEMNATION AND PAUL'S THORN

Justification is referred to in Bible passages that speak of the Book of Life. When you were born again, your name was written in this Book. It won't be erased if you don't preach the gospel to your neighbor. It doesn't matter if you believe you failed somehow. Your name will remain in the Lamb's Book of Life. While we remain justified in God's eyes, however, we are still inclined to sin. We are dependent upon God through His Spirit to sanctify us in those areas. As we strive to be holy as God is holy, we need His help to aim for that goal.

Many years ago, a certain holiness teaching dictated that church leadership should instruct their congregants on how to live and what to do. If they followed the dictates of the church, they would become holy. This became known as the Holiness Movement. It promoted a very legalistic way of living. If you do good things and live just right you will become holy. Trying to live a "holy life" is challenging, however, and leads to feelings of failure and condemnation. As a result, a large number left the church and returned to a worldly lifestyle. Many who remained were convinced they had become sanctified and no longer sinned.

I once worked with a man who had been in the Holiness Movement. Thankfully, he realizes now that he hasn't "arrived." Sometimes I think he's close because in many ways he seems to be a better person than I am. Regardless of where either one of us is in our walk as a believer, we remain equally justified in God's eyes. It doesn't matter if I am the worst person in the world or the best, because all have sinned and fall short of the glory of God (Romans 3:23). Everyone requires the blood of the Lamb to be justified.

Regarding sanctification, however, each one of us is in a different place. Depending on where we are in our walk with God, He works with each of us in His own way and in His own time. I'm not where you are, and you aren't where I am. I have had different spiritual growth experiences than you. That's neither good nor bad; it's just something to remember when you see another believer "doing something I would never do because I know it's wrong in God's eyes." Stop and bring your nose down a notch. The other believer is experiencing his own walk with the Lord. God does not think any less of him for his actions. Both of you are considered righteous.

Condemnation and Conviction

When condemnation arises because of an inappropriately spoken word or action, how do you determine its source? Is God wanting to change you, or is the devil trying to pull you down? To answer that question, we will investigate the difference between condemnation and conviction.

Condemnation deems that you are unfit and worthless. It offers no hope and makes you miserable. It may drive you to consider standing in the middle of the interstate on a dark, moonless night. That would be a radical action, but hopelessness can easily drive one to acts of desperation. Condemnation is utterly lifeless, discouraging, and full of death and shame. It is always directed *at the person*. This doesn't sound like the God of love who constantly invites us to come close to Him. Know with certainty that God, through His Spirit, will *never* condemn you. Ever. But He will *convict* you as a part of the sanctification process. Conviction arises when the Holy Spirit wants to change something in your life, and it will always arrive with hope. It will contain loving words wrapped with hope and mercy as He works in you. When you cooperate with Him, He will begin to transform the area He has pointed out to you. It will be a loving experience, like a tender father teaching his beloved son. Conviction will be directed *at the poor decision, or action*. It may be uncomfortable, but with it, He will always offer hope and life. You will know in your spirit that God is right, and you will discover that you want to work with Him to change your actions and thoughts. You will feel good inside. If you experience condemnation at any point in this process, tell the devil you are no longer open to condemnation. Yield yourself wholly to the work of the Spirit. "God, I am open to Your conviction."

I experience condemnation occasionally because I am not on the street every day preaching the gospel. A little inner voice says, "You don't love people, Marty; you don't care. You're not even a Christian. You're worthless. You'll never get into heaven. You're ashamed of God, aren't you?" Other times that voice will tell me, "You don't pray enough," or, "You'll never be good enough." I'm certain you have heard the same voice at one time or another, speaking the same or similar words. The accuser doesn't give anyone a pass.

The Accuser

In Revelation 12:10 we read, "the accuser of our brothers and sisters... accuses them before our God day and night." The identity of the accuser is none other than Satan, and those he accuses are the believers in Yeshua. He isn't the only one who accuses. Sadly, some in the church believe their calling is to point out the failures and shortcomings of others. Have you run into one of those people? Or have you been that person? When you feel the overpowering urge to correct someone, be very, very careful. If God has not asked you to engage in this activity, you are doing the accuser's job. Now you have the title of "accuser" alongside Satan. Ask God to alert you when you are tempted to speak words of accusation. Then ask Him to help you to be aware of and to participate in the conviction process of the Holy Spirit by lovingly coming alongside the one who is struggling. What a blessed change that would be! The accused person will experience contentment and encouragement instead of hopeless condemnation.

I occasionally become aware of a problem area in someone's life or a sticky situation in the congregation. I always go to God and ask Him what I should do before I approach anyone. If the situation is recurring and may hurt someone, it becomes the responsibility of church leadership and I handle it appropriately. Individual situations, however, are usually laid to rest after I talk to God. He may want the opportunity to work in that person's life. I don't need to be involved. I can let God be God, or I can be an accuser. It should be a simple choice.

In the prophetic realm, it is critical that words of condemnation are never spoken. Paul addressed this in his first letter to the Corinthians:

> But the one who prophesies speaks to people for their strengthening, encouraging and comfort.
> —1 Corinthians 14:3

> But he that prophesieth speaketh unto men to edification, and exhortation, and comfort.
> —1 Corinthians 14:3 (KJV)

There were never to be words of correction in the realm of the prophetic unless the person speaking first gained approval from church leadership. Next, he was to go to the person to whom the prophetic word was to be addressed and seek permission to speak. The same holds true today. Prophetic words should encourage, build faith, or bring comfort.

When the accuser condemns you, turn to God and ask Him to take the pain of that condemnation away. Pray. Put on your armor and use the weapons of spiritual warfare to fight the enemy (Ephesians 6:10–18). Encourage yourself in His presence and in His Word. Ask the Lord to bring to you His conviction and let Him know you are open to it in His timing.

A Further Look at Justification

Yeshua told Nicodemus that no one can see the kingdom of God unless he is born again (John 3:3). Nicodemus, a righteous Pharisee, was mystified. There are several born-again experiences in Judaism, and Nicodemus, being a teacher of rabbis, had experienced all of them. This was why he asked Yeshua if it was necessary to start over (enter his mother's womb), since being a Jew was the first experience. But Yeshua was speaking something else.

> Jesus answered, "Very truly I tell you, no one can enter the kingdom of God unless they are born of water and the Spirit. Flesh gives birth to flesh, but the Spirit gives birth to spirit. You should not be surprised at my saying, 'You must be born again.' The wind blows wherever it pleases. You hear its sound, but you cannot tell where it comes from or where it is going. So it is with everyone born of the Spirit."
> —John 3:5–8

When Yeshua said you must be "born of the Spirit," He was speaking of the New Covenant that He would establish in the near future. It had nothing to do with Nicodemus' previous experiences.

> Just as Moses lifted up the snake in the wilderness, so the Son of Man must be lifted up, that everyone who believes may have eternal life in him." For God so loved the world that he gave his one and only Son, that whoever believes in him shall not perish but have eternal life. For God did not send his Son into the world to condemn the world, but to save the world through him.
> —John 3:14–17

Yeshua was addressing justification in this passage. When reading it in context, it is clear anyone who believed in the Son of Man (Yeshua), the One who would be "lifted up" (on the cross), would be "born again." The one who placed their faith in the blood of Jesus would be justified, made righteous.

More About Conviction and Sanctification

One is made righteous by the blood of Yeshua, then sanctified by the Holy Spirit and the Word. When Yeshua prayed for His disciples, He asked His Father to "sanctify them by the tı your word is truth." (See John 17:17.)

Paul also addressed sanctification:

> He gave me the priestly duty of proclaiming the gospel of God, so that the Gentiles might become an offering acceptable to God, sanctified by the Holy Spirit.
> —Romans 15:16

> You were washed, you were sanctified, you were justified in the name of the Lord Jesus Christ and by the Spirit of our God.
> —1 Corinthians 6:11

As I previously stated, the Spirit of God convicts when He wants to address a specific issue in a believer's life. There will be no condemnation; He will simply point out what He wants to change. Then, with the cooperation of the believer, He will begin the process of change in the area He has targeted. To illustrate, I'll use a situation from my own life.

Our church's dance ministry participates in several parades each year. A couple of years ago we took our position in a parade's set-up area and began to check the sound system. We turned the volume way up to test it, then turned it back down and let the music continue to play in the background. A few members of the dance team were stretching in preparation for the upcoming mile-long dance and others were talking. Nearby, other parade participants were making their own preparations. Suddenly, I noticed a woman separate herself from the group next to ours. She walked toward us with a look of grim determination. Stopping in front of me, she announced in a hostile voice that our music was way too loud and was hurting everyone's ears. Ironically, she and I were talking in normal everyday voices as we stood next to the speaker. If the music had been too loud, we wouldn't have been able to hear each other. Frankly, I didn't see how our music could be hurting anyone's ears, close to the speaker or not. With all this running through my mind, I told her, "Well, it's going to get a lot louder before we're finished." That set her off. She let loose with a tirade of angry words. One of the many things she threw at me was the threat of a lawsuit. When she'd had her say, she swung around and marched back to her group, shoulders stiff, chin thrust forward. She got in the convertible at the front of her group, and with a stony face stared straight ahead.

I knew our music wasn't too loud. Perhaps this woman disliked Christian music. Maybe she didn't like Christians, or maybe she was angry at God because of something that had occurred in her life. I dismissed the incident from my mind and turned back to our group. Everything went along quite smoothly for about 20 minutes, when *boom!* The Holy Spirit suddenly showed up. It was conviction time. I smiled because I knew this was going to hurt, but it would be a "good" hurt. I responded immediately. "I know, Lord, I know. I just need five minutes and then I'll go talk to the woman." I wasn't experiencing condemnation. I knew it was conviction. The Holy Spirit wanted me to talk to the offended woman because the testimony of the Lord was at stake. She may have been sitting in her car thinking, "Yep, that man is just like all those other Christians. That's why I hate them, because of jerks like him." Those may not have been her exact thoughts, but whatever she was thinking, I wouldn't be shown in a positive light.

I took a deep breath and approached the woman. I stood by the car door for a moment as the woman stared straight ahead and refused to acknowledge me. I glanced at the steering wheel and saw she was gripping it so hard that I thought it might bend. I felt myself becoming apprehensive and wondered what my fate would be if she got out of the car. Would I have to run? I took a deep breath, looked at her, and said, "Hey." Her eyes flashed daggers as she looked up at me. I held her gaze and said very simply, "I'm sorry." Instantly, the steely-faced woman transformed before my eyes into a completely different person. The expression on her face softened and her grip on the steering wheel relaxed. She replied, "Oh, well, thank you." I didn't think it necessary to say anything else, so I patted her shoulder, turned, and walked back to our group.

As the Holy Spirit convicted me about my words and attitude in response to the woman's initial approach, I made the decision to cooperate with the Spirit and apologize. If I ever see the woman again, maybe we will approach each other as good friends. It appeared all hard feelings had been resolved, and I am certain it was because God was involved. I had made the decision to let God be God. That's all He asks. Respond to His conviction, and let Him do His work.

God's conviction doesn't always occur the moment a person acts outside of God's will, as in the last illustration. I once attended a Sunday night service where the pastor taught from Acts 15. I had never heard anyone teach about being set free from the Law. While the pastor spoke, I began to sense God's conviction. He gently told me that I needed to die to my own self. This had nothing to do with what I had said or done against anyone. God was simply exposing the way I was living my life. And it felt good. We need to understand that when God convicts, He is ready to help. He is not in the business of convicting someone and then leaving him high and dry. I will never hear God say, "Go figure it out, Marty." There are a lot of things I don't like about myself, but I am helpless to change any of them on my own. I can try, but ultimately it won't work. I'll end up under condemnation, and it will literally suck the last bit of life out of me. It will rob me of the opportunity to participate with God in the sanctification process.

I love what Paul said about this in his second letter to the Corinthians:

> He has made us competent as ministers of a new covenant—not of the letter but of the Spirit; for the letter kills, but the Spirit gives life.
> —2 Corinthians 3:6

CHAPTER 1: NO CONDEMNATION AND PAUL'S THORN

When condemnation knocks at your door and the words you hear in your spirit have absolutely no life, reject them immediately. They are not from God. On the other hand, words of conviction will come with life, joy, and hope. Embrace them and invite the Spirit to do His life-changing, life-giving work of sanctification.

> Now the Lord is the Spirit, and where the Spirit of the Lord is, there is freedom. And we all, who with unveiled faces contemplate the Lord's glory, are being transformed into his image with ever-increasing glory, which comes from the Lord, who is the Spirit.
> —2 Corinthians 3:17–18

The word "transformed" in this verse is the Greek word *metamorphoō*, meaning to change into another form, or to be transformed. It's where we get our word "metamorphosis." A beautiful example of *metamorphoō* is seen in the life cycle of a butterfly. It begins as an egg, changes to a larva (caterpillar), then to a pupa (chrysalis or cocoon), until finally a beautiful butterfly emerges. From beginning to end, the butterfly is being continually transformed. Just like the butterfly, followers of Yeshua are continually transformed as they cooperate with the Holy Spirit in the sanctification process. Paul goes even further and says there is glory in this process, an ever-increasing glory. Hallelujah!

There is another aspect to conviction that is important to understand. When God wants to change someone, He won't attack an issue that is contrary to His will for that person. As an example, let's say I eat too much ice cream, scoops of it every day. Because I am not being a good steward of my body, God convicts me by pointing out that I need to change my habits. He won't cause the ice cream delivery man to have a flat tire so he can't deliver ice cream to me. God doesn't deal with the external aspects of an issue. Rather, He will go straight to the heart. That is what He wants to change. Jeremiah 17:9 says the heart is deceitful above all things and is desperately wicked, and who can know it? That, in a nutshell, is me. And it is you. Because our hearts have a sin nature, we are desperately wicked. What does God do? He performs heart surgery. He literally transforms our hearts. If I listen to the conviction of the Holy Spirit regarding my ice cream intake, and if I submit myself to His direction and work with Him, my heart will change. I will be a different person. It's not that I will exercise more self-control for the sake of exerting self-control alone. Rather, my heart will be changed. I may continue to desire ice cream, but I will be able to make the decision to eat less of it because I have become different on the inside. The ice cream delivery man won't be seeing me nearly as often, and he won't have to worry about a flat tire on his way to my house.

The New Covenant that Yeshua established is altogether a matter of the heart. The externals of the Mosaic Covenant, like Shabbat laws, kosher food, and offering sacrifices, were dropped with the establishment of the New Covenant. The New Covenant amplified the internal aspects of the Law. The Old Covenant commanded, "Thou shalt not murder." Under the New Covenant, Yeshua said there should not even be the *desire* to murder. The Old Covenant said not to commit adultery. Under the New Covenant, one is guilty of adultery if he even *thinks* about committing the act. The New Covenant is much harder to keep, and to do so one has to undergo a heart change. You can be a rotten person and keep the old outward Law, but you can't be a rotten person and keep New Covenant law. Because living under the New Covenant is a matter of the heart, you must be filled with the love of God in the person of Jesus Christ by the Holy Spirit. It is here that the Spirit's conviction can open the door to transformation.

David cried out to God in Psalm 51:10, "Create in me a pure heart, O God." David didn't tell himself to create the new heart. It would have been impossible for him to do so, just as it is for you and me. The only way anyone can obtain a pure heart is to go before God and say, "O God, change my heart." Only then will the Holy Spirit begin His work of sanctification to transform a person's heart.

What is the state of you heart? Do you find yourself crying out like David, "Create in me a pure heart, O God?" If so, listen to the words of conviction the Holy Spirit speaks to you. Allow Him to access your heart so He can begin transforming your life. It will be a wonderful, life-changing decision.

Paul's Thorn

Why discuss Paul's thorn in the middle of a chapter on condemnation? It may seem odd, but as we proceed, we will discover there is a strong connection between the two.

You have undoubtedly heard pastors teach on the many different analyses of Paul's thorn. I've heard my share, but I have yet to hear anyone teach what I am about to pass on to you. We'll have some fun, but I give you fair warning. Hold on and fasten your seat belts.

> To keep me from becoming conceited because of these surpassingly great revelations, there was given me a thorn in my flesh, a messenger of Satan, to torment me. Three times I pleaded with the Lord to take it away from me. But he said to me, "My grace is sufficient for you, for my power is made perfect in weakness." Therefore I will boast all the more gladly about my weaknesses, so that Christ's power may rest on me.
> —2 Corinthians 12:7–9

Like you, I have always heard we don't know with certainty what Paul's thorn in the flesh was. After lengthy study, however, I have come to a different conclusion. A careful reading of verse seven tells us exactly what the thorn was. "Therefore. . . I was given a thorn in my flesh, a messenger of Satan, to torment me." The thorn was a message, an accusation, from the accuser. It is the specifics of the message that are unclear.

The word "messenger" in the original Greek text refers to one who delivers a report or a declaration. The messenger was sent by Satan, the accuser, to deliver a message to Paul. This message was one of accusation intended to torment Paul ("buffet" in the KJV). *Aggelos* is the Greek word for "angel," meaning "messenger," and *kolaphizo* is the Greek word for "torment," meaning "to beat in the face with fists." This begins to present a picture of what Paul was enduring. The messenger aggressively accused Paul until he was driven to plead with the Lord to remove the torment. The Lord answered that He would not remove the "thorn" because His power would be made perfect in Paul's weakness.

This scenario leads me to believe that the thorn Paul and the Lord were talking about was not a physical ailment. There would be no need to send a messenger to Paul to declare something that would be obvious to him. When you are sick or have a broken arm, you don't need someone to tell you what you already know.

What exactly was in the message that Paul received? Why didn't Paul say what it was? I believe that information was withheld to emphasize the lesson, rather than the content, of the adversary's message. This allows the Holy Spirit to do His work as the entire passage is read. Otherwise, the specifics of the message would be a distraction.

Whatever the message, Paul was not pleased with it. He pleaded with the Lord for the "thorn" to be removed. I've paraphrased the Lord's answer. "Nope, I'm not going to do it." He refused because His power would be "most effective" (Amplified Version) or "made perfect" (NIV) in Paul's weakness. It sounds crazy, but is it?

Clarification is found in the Greek word for power, *dunamis*. The word "dynamite" comes from *dunamis*. Dynamite is highly explosive, and that's the kind of power God wanted to release in Paul through his weakness. What would that have looked like?

Chapter 1: No Condemnation and Paul's Thorn

My twin brother, Mike, and I grew up playing with TNT. Yes, we were a little crazy in our youth. We would purchase dynamite, blasting caps, a length of fuse, what we thought of as "all the good stuff." Today you can't purchase dynamite off the shelf, but it was readily accessible in our youth. When we exploded the dynamite in the open, it didn't do a lot. Yes, it was loud, and we felt a small concussion, but it was no big deal. We also put dynamite in different kinds of containers, lit the fuse and watched spectacular displays of TNT's power. That was the kind of display the Lord wanted in Paul's life. Through the "container" of Paul's weakness, the Lord's *dunamis* power would be displayed in a remarkable way.

God told Paul His *dunamis* was made perfect in weakness. The Greek word for weakness is *astheneia,* meaning a frailty, weakness, or feebleness. One of the definitions of "frailty" is a weakness of character, and to be "feeble-minded" is to lack strength of character. This all boils down to a mental weakness or character flaw, indicating this may have been the accusation against Paul by Satan's messenger. Has the messenger of the accuser ever come to you and said, "You jerk! You idiot! You are just plain no good. Look what you did!" (or "said" or "thought"). I believe this was the type of accusation with which Paul was being soundly beaten.

There is a good side to Paul's situation. In 2 Corinthians 12:7, Paul said he experienced this thorn in the flesh to keep him from becoming conceited. Whatever the character flaw, Paul would stay humble and the Lord's *dunamis* power would be made perfect through it. God wanted to demonstrate His grace and His power through Paul. If the thorn had been removed, Paul may have been more inclined to pursue his ministry through his own power. In fact, Paul said the thorn remained to keep him from becoming conceited or puffed up.

As I studied this passage, the Lord revealed something to me that I believe will bring freedom. As we become more like

Yeshua through the work of the Holy Spirit, understand that we are not God and we will not become like Him this side of Heaven. We will have character flaws as long as we live. Otherwise, we would begin to think we were really something. No wonder Paul said, "In order to keep me from becoming conceited. . ." If you want God's power in your life, stay in a "faulted" position with the understanding that you are not God. Allow Him to remain on the throne. When the serpent tempted Eve with the fruit of the Tree of Knowledge, he said, "When you eat from it your eyes will be opened, and you will be like God, knowing good and evil." (Genesis 3:5.) All sin originates from the same place, the prideful desire to be like God. When you take this attitude and begin to think you are something mighty good, you set yourself up for a big fall. The Lord will back off. "I can't work with you. I can't give you grace or power." Self-righteousness is a killer.

When the Lord refused Paul's request to remove the thorn, Paul finally had a revelation and reversed his position. "Oh! You mean if I don't have to deal with condemnation about my character and personality faults, then I will lose some of your grace and power, Lord? Well, then, let me boast more gladly about my weakness. If it means I receive more power, more grace, and more of God in my life, then I'm glad I've got faults. This means Messiah's power can rest on me. For Messiah's sake, I delight in my weaknesses, because then I am strong in God's power." Paul no longer desired to have his character flaw removed. He saw victory in letting God be God. Paul could simply be who he was and allow the Lord's power to work in him, rather than depending on his own power. It is critical to understand this point. Just be who you are, faults and all, and allow God's power to work in you. The minute you forget this principle, the Holy Spirit will fly away to find someone else He can use. Instead of being condemned as he was "beat in the face by the fists of accusation," and instead of pleading for God to deliver him from accusation, condemnation, and torment, Paul turned around with a hallelujah. "I'm not God. I have faults, but God does not. That means He's God, and I'm not. Thank you, devil, for reminding me. Thank you because I almost forgot."

If I were faultless, I might think I was like God, and that would place me in a horrible position. I would be just like Satan, the fallen angel who saw himself as God. Instead, I praise God because I have faults, many faults. "Oh God, I understand now, and may that understanding keep me safe from pride, the greatest sin."

While I have taken liberties with what Paul may have been thinking, I do know he rejoiced. In 2 Corinthians 12:9, Paul said he would "boast all the more gladly" about his weaknesses. The Greek word for boast is *kauchaomai,* which means "to glory on account of something." Paul began to glory in his faults. He understood that despite his faults, the Lord would work through him in a powerful way.

Where does this leave the power of condemnation in your life? I have good news. This power does not exist. When condemnation arises, react like Paul did and boast "all the more gladly" about your weakness. Be reminded that God is God and He alone is the perfect One. Rejoice! By turning condemnation into praise, it will have no power over you.

The Other Side

How do you handle a situation that reveals a character flaw in someone else? Do you point your finger, jump quickly to judgment, and condemn that person? While such a response is tempting, begin training yourself to respond with humility instead. "Oh, look! He's just like me. He isn't God, either. Wow! God's going to use him because he's not perfect. Glory hallelujah!" Instead of becoming self-righteous and judgmental, rejoice with him. We know Who God is, we know who the other person is, and we certainly know who we are. This mindset will stop us from taking on Satan's role as accuser and create a safeguard against worshiping others or ourselves.

Pride takes root easily, and it is as dangerous as the dynamite Mike and I used to play with. No matter how careful you are with it, eventually it will blow up in your face. Solomon, the wisest man who ever lived, told us what would happen if pride was allowed a place in our lives.

> He *[the Lord]* mocks proud mockers but shows favor to the humble.
> —Proverbs 3:34

Both James, the brother of Yeshua, and Peter, referenced this verse in their letters.

> God opposes the proud but gives grace to the humble.
> —James 4:6b

> All of you, clothe yourselves with humility toward one another, because, "God opposes the proud but gives grace to the humble.
> —1 Peter 5:5

Recognize and glory in your faults. Otherwise, the age-old struggle with pride will grow and take over your life. The verses above make it clear what happens next. God will oppose you. There goes the dynamite. Not in a good way this time. You don't want God to take a stand against you. Recognize your faults and humble yourself before God. He will lift you up and give you grace. Send the dynamite back. Or better yet, hand it to the accuser himself, Satan.

Chapter 1: No Condemnation and Paul's Thorn

When the accuser comes with an accusation, you have a choice. Plead with God for deliverance, or do what Paul did and rejoice in that weakness:

> That is why, for Christ's sake, I delight in weaknesses, in insults, in hardships, in persecutions, in difficulties. For when I am weak, then I am strong.
> —2 Corinthians 12:10

The Greek word for "rejoice" in this verse is *eudokeō,* to "take pleasure" in something. Paul said, "This is why, for Christ's sake, I take pleasure in weaknesses. . ." What a revelation! Take pleasure in your faults. It will act as a safety valve for you and keep you humble.

Mike and I worked at the Fort Saint Vrain Generating Station near Platteville, Colorado, when it was a nuclear power plant. We openly declared our faith, and we started a church there. It had good attendance, but there were a few who opposed us. One man mocked me incessantly for being a Christian. He was a big macho guy who was into martial arts. It seemed like he hated me, and I'm convinced his favorite sport was making fun of me. One day we both got on the elevator to go down to the reactor. There were others on the elevator with us, so I wasn't too worried. I was wrong on that count. After the elevator door closed, this big man grabbed me and put me in a sleeper choke hold. I struggled to free myself as he laughed and continued to hold me. I wasn't laughing. The experience was painful and humiliating.

Later, the same man and I worked together on a steam valve below the reactor. After a short conversation I said, "The Lord wants you. He just wants you." He turned abruptly, walked around the reactor, and left the area. His actions didn't surprise me as he was offended frequently by something I said. I continued my work and finished the job. Later, he approached me and said something that rendered me speechless. After he left me at the reactor that day, he had gone to his office where he prayed and received Yeshua as his Lord and Savior. Hallelujah!

About a month later my former tormenter approached me and said he had become involved in a church. I was excited for him. As he spoke, however, it became clear he had joined a church that was part of the Holiness Movement. He was convinced that by doing good things he would become more and more holy. In fact, he believed he was very close to being like God. My heart plummeted, and all I could do was pray that the Holy Spirit would reveal the truth to him.

A few years ago, I went to a meeting at the power plant where I saw this man. I struck up a conversation with him and asked how he was doing. Much to my dismay, I learned he was no longer associated with any church. He had returned to a worldly lifestyle. While his departure from living a Christian life could be for any number of reasons, one thing I know with certainty. The mentality of doing good things to be accepted by God is a dangerous way to live. It leads directly to a self-righteous attitude that lends itself to finger-pointing and judgment. I'm not saying we shouldn't fight the good fight of faith and do all we can, but we should be aware of who we are and who God is. Let the voice of accusation remind you only of your weakness, and glory in that weakness. Allow God's power to rest upon you and in you as He uses you in ministry to others. Not by your power, but by God's.

Conclusion

When the accuser comes to you with words of accusation and condemnation, decide today what your response will be. Will you plead with God to remove the fault that his condemnation exposes? Will you turn the tables on Satan and say, "Thank you for reminding me that I am not God?" In making the latter decision, you can rejoice in the fact that you know you are not God. The power of accusation will be removed, and the power of God can rest upon you and in you. You won't think too highly of yourself, and you won't be tempted to judge other people. Having humbled yourself before God, He will show you favor

CHAPTER 1: NO CONDEMNATION AND PAUL'S THORN

and lift you up. His power will come upon you to fulfill the work He has planned for you.

There you have it—the thorn in the flesh. You are not God. Hallelujah! As I was in prayer earlier this week, a wave of condemnation arose because of something I had said a few days before. "Oh yes. Thank you for reminding me I'm not God. I have faults, but I know the One who has no faults." I turned from condemnation and began praising Him, for He alone *is* God. I slammed the door on the accuser and Messiah was glorified.

Thank you, Lord God, for being God. Thank You for reminding me that I am not God, and that everything must be in You. I cannot place any trust in myself. I am open now to Your power and Your grace. Amen.

Chapter 2:

The Prodigal Son

Almost everyone is familiar with the phrase, "The prodigal has returned." Many associate these words with the Bible story of the prodigal son. Others are reminded of a family member who left home and later returned. For our purposes, we will consider the actual definition of a prodigal, a person who spends his money recklessly and in a wasteful manner. We can deduce a prodigal is one who lives life recklessly beyond his means and gives no thought to tomorrow. He believes life is meant to be lived today while plans for tomorrow can wait. Ultimately, a prodigal favors enjoyable pursuit over more serious endeavors.

As we study The Parable of the Prodigal Son, we will see that he is presented this way. We may consider him good for nothing, but there are many lessons buried within his story. The same can be said about his father's and older brother's actions. As we explore the parable and the language and customs of the day, we will uncover many surprises.

My Bible introduces this story as "The Parable of the Lost Son." It could have been titled "The Story of the Two Sons," or "The Story of the Father." None of these titles, however, come close to describing what Yeshua wished to impart to His listeners. This story is incredibly intense. It contains layer upon layer of truth, and it packs a mountain of meaning within a very short message.

It is important to understand that Yeshua's parables are not intended to be taken literally. In addition, the layers of understanding included in them are not easily discovered. The Parable of the Wheat and the Tares in Matthew 13:24–30 easily makes this point. A man sowed good seed in his field. While he slept, the enemy came and sowed tares among the wheat, tares being another word for weeds. Both kinds of seed sprouted and grew in the same field. Eventually the weeds became obvious to the owner's servants, and they approached the owner to ask if he wanted the weeds pulled. The owner knew that when the weeds were pulled some of the wheat would be pulled loose as well. He told his servants to let the wheat and tares grow together until it was time for harvest, then pull the weeds, bundle them, and burn them. After that the wheat was to be gathered into the owner's barn.

Yeshua wasn't speaking of literal wheat and tares. The parable had an underlying message that He later explained to his disciples (Matthew 13:36–43). The owner of the field was the Son of Man, Yeshua. The field was the world. The good seed represented the people of the kingdom. The weeds were the people of the evil one, and the enemy who sowed them was the devil. The harvest represented the end of the age, and the harvesters were angels. The parable illustrated the end of the age, but that message would be received only by those who discerned it. "Whoever has ears," Yeshua said, "let them hear."

Open your ears to the underlying message in The Parable of the Prodigal Son. Guard yourself against getting stuck on obvious details. This may sound daunting, especially when surface matters are easily seen. One method to gain insight into a parable's underlying message is to study the original biblical text. It's helpful to have a concordance on hand to research the meaning of key Greek words. In addition, the reader should consult resources and commentaries that explain the customs of Yeshua's day. These steps will lead to a much deeper understanding of the parable's truths, especially when combined with prayerful meditation.

Utilizing these methods of study, I examined The Parable of the Lost Son and discovered a trove of information. It wasn't long before I became convinced I would have at least ten messages relating to the parable. I mentioned this to a fellow pastor who looked at me in disbelief. She told me it would be impossible to dig so much information from such a short parable. Much to my delight and satisfaction, I did have ten messages when I concluded my study.

As I made my way through what appeared to be a mountain of resources, I discovered that many Bible scholars have explored The Parable of the Lost Son. Some said the older son in the parable represented Israel and the younger son represented the church. While this is a widely accepted interpretation in today's Messianic movement, other scholars have held the opposite view. I found most interpretations were quite subjective. The majority, however, agreed that the parable contained many elements. They included love, compassion, mercy, misery, judgment, life, and joy.

The main characters in the parable are the father and his two sons. Most of the action centers on these three men. We will uncover many lessons by observing their interaction. Another character is the Observer. He appears in various guises. He may be a farm hand, a servant, or even a guest. The latter is an easy role because he watches events unfold without participating in them. His heart is protected, and potential hurts are avoided. Like watching a game from the sidelines, the Observer identifies with his team but takes no part in the action. Many believers play this role quite well, convinced it is safer to remain uninvolved. Their motto is "No obligation, no risk, and no pain." It's all about security. While the Observer remains protected, at the end of the day he will find himself in "Nowheresville," still sitting on the sidelines.

I mention this because I want to caution you not to be the Observer as you read this parable. You may be sorely tempted, especially if this is your default role in everyday life. The best way to learn from the story is to take an active part in it. Identify with each of the main characters. As you become one with them in their roles, allow God to speak to you through them. The truth embedded in the story will change you. Open your heart, invite the Holy Spirit to speak to you, and give yourself permission to experience deliverance, healing, and transformation.

When I began studying The Parable of the Lost Son, I chose to stay on the sidelines as an Observer. I was especially interested in the younger son. What was his attitude as he decided to leave home? I also wanted to see how the father handled his son's heart-wrenching decision. How did he deal with his son's long absence and his sudden return? Fascinated with how each one would react, I settled into what I thought would be a comfortable role and cruised through my daily study. This worked very well for a short time. In His mercy, God taught me many truths as I studied. Then one day He jolted me out of my comfort zone. To my absolute and utter astonishment, I realized I was the lost younger son. I would like to say that I accepted the revelation and immediately changed my ways, but such a statement would be far from the truth. The process of accepting what God showed me was slow, and so was letting go of my nice safe role as Observer. I finally humbled myself before the Lord and allowed myself to become vulnerable. It was there that I discovered a unique beauty in presence of God. I urge you to do likewise as the Holy Spirit speaks to you through this study. Step out of your safe observation box, let go of the status quo, and draw close to God as we proceed.

Those of us who live in observation bubbles have found them quite safe and very comfortable. Venturing too deeply into personal relationships with others or even with God is out of the question. The day will arrive, however, when we watch others walk in God's blessings and wonder why we aren't being blessed. We'll notice the friend who was totally messed up has now become compassionate and kind, with a genuine love for others. He used to be an unhappy nervous wreck, but now he is joyful and at peace. He tells you God has changed him, and you ask yourself why God hasn't changed you. The answer is simple, but the same may not be said about the action required to accept the answer. You must become vulnerable before YHVH[1] before He can accomplish His work in you. Cooperate with the Spirit as He begins your transformation process. Becoming vulnerable is scary, but it's a necessary step.

Such an undertaking is not without its struggles. It often requires extending forgiveness to someone who has hurt you, or receiving it from someone you have hurt. Though difficult, the former is often easier. When it comes to receiving forgiveness, especially from God, it's easy to become resistant. A sense of unworthiness takes on mountainous proportions as pride rears its ugly head. We strive to earn God's forgiveness. "I'll go to church more often—every Sunday morning, noon, and night," you tell God. You list the good things you will do for the widow down the street, for the single mom or dad at church, and anyone else who comes to mind. You'll determine to be more kind. When you finally take a breath, you'll discover you have created a long mental list of things you will do to gain God's favor and forgiveness.

When it comes to receiving anything from God, forgiveness included, we need to come to a place of surrender before Him. We won't earn His forgiveness by striving to be a better person. Instead, we must yield ourselves to God and allow Him to love

---

[1] The tetragrammaton, YHVH, is the four-letter name of God. It consists of the Hebrew consonants yod, hey, vov, hey, commonly transcribed into English as YHVH. The tetragrammaton is known as The Name or, as Jews would say, Ha Shem.

us unconditionally. Trust in His love, and simply receive His forgiveness.

The Parable of the Prodigal Son

Jesus continued: "There was a man who had two sons. The younger one said to his father, 'Father, give me my share of the estate.' So he divided his property between them. Not long after that, the younger son got together all he had, set off for a distant country and there squandered his wealth in wild living. After he had spent everything, there was a severe famine in that whole country, and he began to be in need. So he went and hired himself out to a citizen of that country, who sent him to his fields to feed pigs. He longed to fill his stomach with the pods that the pigs were eating, but no one gave him anything. When he came to his senses, he said, 'How many of my father's hired servants have food to spare, and here I am starving to death! I will set out and go back to my father and say to him: Father, I have sinned against heaven and against you. I am no longer worthy to be called your son; make me like one of your hired servants.' So he got up and went to his father. But while he was still a long way off, his father saw him and was filled with compassion for him; he ran to his son, threw his arms around him and kissed him. The son said to him, 'Father, I have sinned against heaven and against you. I am no longer worthy to be called your son.' But the father said to his servants, 'Quick! Bring the best robe and put it on him. Put a ring on his finger and sandals on his feet. Bring the fattened calf and kill it. Let's have a feast and celebrate. For this son of mine was dead and is alive again; he was lost and is found.' So they began to celebrate. Meanwhile, the older son was in the field. When he came near the house, he heard music and dancing. So he called one of the servants and asked him what was going on. 'Your brother has come,' he replied, 'and your father has killed the fattened calf because he has him back safe and sound.' The older brother became angry and refused to go in. So his

father went out and pleaded with him. But he answered his father, 'Look! All these years I've been slaving for you and never disobeyed your orders. Yet you never gave me even a young goat so I could celebrate with my friends. But when this son of yours who has squandered your property with prostitutes comes home, you kill the fattened calf for him!' 'My son,' the father said, 'you are always with me, and everything I have is yours. But we had to celebrate and be glad, because this brother of yours was dead and is alive again; he was lost and is found.'"
—Luke 15:11–31

What a welcome the lost son received! After a prolonged absence, he returned to an unexpectedly enthusiastic reception. While we rejoice with both the father and the son, we must not fail to examine the emotions the father experienced when his son departed.

The circumstances surrounding the son's departure were anything but pleasant. Shockingly, the son had demanded from his father his future inheritance. Such a request went against every custom and tradition of Yeshua's day. Distribution of an inheritance took place only after the father's death. By making such an offensive request, the son could have been severely beaten. He could have been cut from the family with no inheritance and thrown out of the house.

When the son made his shocking demand, his father would have stared in disbelief. His beloved son insisted on a division of the estate and the right to spend his share immediately. In effect he said, "I can't wait for you to die, dad. I really wish you were dead now, but since you're not, go ahead and give me my money. I can't wait years and years for it." The son was rejecting his home, his father's way of life, and the land of his birth. The father was surely considering the implications of all he had heard. Finally, contrary to everyone's expectations and against all customs of the day, the father gave the rebellious son his future inheritance.

Out of love, the father chose to act outside the norms of the day. The son, with no love flowing out of his heart, had his own selfish plan. In Bible times, it was customary to remain near family throughout life. When children married, they often lived on family land where everyone could care for one another and share responsibilities. In this case, home was not where the son's heart was. He wanted to experience a different kind of life, and he needed to be far away from Dad's influence so he could do as he pleased.

The father, heartbroken, devastated, and crushed, pushed through his sorrow and continually hoped for his son's return. Day after day, month after month, he waited, always with anticipation in his heart. Each morning he hoped to see his son before the sun went down. Finally, one day as he gazed toward the horizon, he saw in the hazy distance a figure plodding down the dusty road. As he watched he suddenly realized it was his son. Incredibly, his son was walking toward him. His heart in his throat, the father's anguish was instantly transformed into a flood of immense joy.

When I teach this parable, I often act out the father's role. I walk back and forth before the audience as I explain that I am actively looking for my missing son. Rather than lying on a couch depressed because my son is missing, I pace back and forth at the fence line of my property and gaze into the distance. Day after day I hope to see my beloved son. One bright, sunny day as I scan the horizon, I notice a man with a familiar walk. "Why, he walks just like me. Surely my son has returned." Laughing and weeping at the same time, I jump over the fence and run toward my son. When I finally meet him, I nearly knock him down as I wrap him in my arms. What joy I experience. What joy the father in the parable experienced! The missing son had come home!

Perhaps you have endured the heartbreak of a child running away from home. Words cannot express the depths of the sorrow and hurt you endured. But when your child returned, and I pray that he did, what indescribable joy you experienced! Likewise, when we turn away from our Father God, His heart breaks as He yearns for our return, and He is overjoyed when we return.

As we read of the prodigal son leaving his home and later returning, we see the picture of a backslider who turned away from his faith and later returned to it. This is one application we can apply to the younger son in our parable. We can also say he represents a sinner who has never known Yeshua and "comes home" to His Father for salvation. Both are plausible, and you may identify with either application.

I was ten years old when I first came home to the Lord. The experience completely changed me. Everyone noticed the transformation. Wild and crazy Marty was suddenly not as wild and crazy. As I entered my teen and young-adult years I had many opportunities to "leave home." Years passed and I did eventually turn away from God. I found myself with the drinking and partying crowd. I returned to the wild and crazy way of living that I had once been known for. Many months later I began to feel that something was missing in my life. I considered returning to God. Those thoughts led to an ongoing mental battle and I became even more miserable. On one side I battled God, and on the other I battled my personal demons. It was like living in a very uncomfortable foxhole. My socks were wet, so to speak, and I felt like my life had smelly mold growing on it. What should I do? I had turned my back on God and done terrible things, and if I surrendered to Him, I knew I would fail and be miserable all over again. It would be far easier to stay in a bar where I knew how to act.

One night I ended up alone in a very dark alley, the battle still raging in my mind. Suddenly, I'd had enough. I was ready to surrender. I laid everything out before God, every dirty rotten thing, and then I recommitted my life to Him. I'd love to say I was instantaneously changed, but that was not the case. It turns out the transformation Yeshua had in mind for me would take some time. While I wanted to be considered a part of God's family, I still felt like a filthy, smelly, dirty sinner. This created a big obstacle in my mind. I wasn't worthy to be God's son. I told Him I would be happy to be His servant. If things worked out down the road, perhaps He would accept me as His son. I took a mental step back and waited to see what He would do with all my "unworthiness."

I didn't have to wait very long. It was my wife who played an integral part in how I heard from God. As I began testing the waters in my new relationship with God, my wife Joan began attending Resurrection Fellowship in Loveland. One Sunday I took what I considered a big risk and stepped into church with my wife. Entering the sanctuary, I walked directly to the row of chairs against the back wall. I figured it would be a safe place to observe everything with the benefit of a quick escape route. I mentally patted myself on my back, satisfied that all my bases were covered. Praise and worship began, and I stood while everyone around me sang and clapped. It sounded very nice, and I decided being in church again wasn't too bad. When the worship portion of the service concluded, I settled into my chair and checked out my "emergency" exits as the pastor began to speak. To this day I can't tell you what he said, but I recall the moment when the consuming love of God suddenly overcame me. Overwhelmed, I wept silently as my mind buzzed with "why" and "how" questions. I was convinced God could not possibly receive me, yet there He was showering me with what felt like a beautiful cleansing rain. Shouldn't I be required to offer ten years of service, or something equally difficult, before He could love me? I still smelled like an ugly hangover, yet there I sat engulfed in the bottomless sea of God's love.

My story, while unique to me, had been told two thousand years ago. Like me, when the son in our parable decided to return home, he still smelled like the pigs he had been feeding. Just as God poured His love over me, the father in our parable showered his son with love. Disregarding the reeking stench that surrounded his son, he lovingly wrapped the young man in his arms. Indeed, a father's love is amazing.

As the prodigal son experienced the warmth and comfort of his father's love, every word he had rehearsed flew out of his mind. The only spoken words came from his father as he directed the servants to kill the fattened calf. He told them to bring a ring, the best robe, and sandals, and they were to put them all on his son. Before the day was over, a celebration would be held to honor his son's return. Undoubtedly, the son's mind was filled with "why" and "how" questions as he struggled to receive his welcome.

The son in Yeshua's parable had returned to his father and received unconditional love. I experienced the same when I returned to my Father God. I was filled with joy and felt refreshingly clean. I was still confused, but I could not deny the reality of what had happened. How quickly my Father God received me, His lost son. Quickly the father in the parable received his lost son. Likewise, God will receive you without hesitation when you find yourself in the same position. Did you at one time ask Yeshua to be your Lord and Savior only to wander away and find yourself living with pigs? Are you tired of the way you smell? My friend, turn to God and He will welcome you back with open arms, no matter what repulsive odor surrounds you.

Having physically left his father, the son in our parable returned. Yeshua presented a beautiful picture of how God receives us when we turn back to Him. We can perceive this lesson as we read the parable on a surface level. But Yeshua had much more to impart. Ultimately, His point was not about a physical event. When a believer denies he belongs to the Father or denies his sonship, he leaves home in a spiritual sense. He may believe God no longer loves him. As a result, he will seek to find the love he desires elsewhere. The believer didn't physically pack his clothes, cell phone, and laptop, and walk out the door of God's house. Rather, he left his spiritual home. The believer rejected the fact God created him, knit him together, and made him a wonderful creation. He began to search for a new home. He may eventually realize that his true home is with His Father God. It will be only in His presence that he will experience God's hand upon him, hear His voice, and find a place of love and acceptance. Intimate words will be spoken into his spirit, and God's plans for him will be revealed.

Are you searching for acceptance from someone other than your Father God? Are you the lost son searching outside your Father's house for love and acceptance? If you are looking to your pastor for satisfaction, he won't be able to provide it. Your church, your teacher, your employer, or your girlfriend or boyfriend can't provide it. Looking in the wrong places will send you on a never-ending search. You will find yourself surrounded by the same stench the prodigal son carried. It is impossible for the world to provide the unconditional acceptance and love that your Father God has for you.

I admit that I sometimes struggle with looking to the world for acceptance. I especially struggle where my ministry is concerned, and feelings of inadequacy arise out of nowhere. When I take my eyes off of my Father even for a short time, I find myself pondering endlessly and fruitlessly why my ministry isn't more successful, at least by my own definition of success. I enviously compare our dance team to other groups who dance at large events. Why wasn't our dance team invited? We are every bit as good, if not better.

Comparison games are never worthwhile. I know because I have engaged in many of them. I must remind myself to redirect my focus away from what I want for my ministry and listen for God's direction. Besides, if I constantly strive to attain a more prestigious status in the church world for the dance ministry, a host of new problems will arise. As I develop an intimate relationship with my Father God, I will begin to experience the unconditional love and acceptance I deeply desire. As I allow His hands to rest on me, I cease striving and find peace and rest. My ministry is wholly accepted by God, and I am as well.

The long-lost son in our parable found rest when his father's hands were placed upon his shoulders. As he found himself engulfed in his father's loving embrace, peace poured over him. "This is home, where you belong," his father might have said. Yeshua presented a beautiful picture of His Father when He told this parable. He longed for His audience to understand the true character of God and to grasp His unconditional love for each one of them.

Although the picture of a loving Father was presented to His listeners, few of them saw God in this light. Given the customs of the day, many would have disagreed with Yeshua's portrayal of the father's welcome. For them, justice and fairness would have been the focus of the parable. They would have felt the son should have been severely punished, maybe even stoned. At the very least, justice demanded that he be disowned. Most of Yeshua's audience would have expected such justice to have been included in the parable. Should you find yourself in agreement with them, take a moment to consider your Father God in the same light. Is there something in your life for which you deserve a just punishment from God? I'll go out on a limb and say you could make a long list. Thankfully, God doesn't punish us as we deserve. Instead, Yeshua willingly paid the price for every sin we could possibly commit, and our Father God opens His arms to us in an expression of unconditional love, mercy, and grace. Our condition doesn't matter to Him. As we approach Him with trust, He will accept us.

Few of Yeshua's listeners believed God would extend such mercy to them. Rather, they perceived God as harsh and judgmental. They were expected to follow numerous religious rules that had major consequences when broken. Yeshua was aware of their beliefs, and He purposely presented the true image of His Father, a loving, merciful, and forgiving Father God. More than one mind would have exploded at the very idea that Almighty God would be so gracious.

The Lord said in Isaiah 55:8, "For my thoughts are not your thoughts, neither are your ways my ways." When we examine this verse in context, we find it can apply to one who judges others and wants recompense for wrongs committed against him. Hurt me, and I will hurt you. But this is not how God operates. His ways are much higher than ours. Where we are judgmental and demanding, He is compassionate and forgiving. He operates in *chesed,* or lovingkindness, and He always exhibits unconditional love. When we fully grasp the magnitude of this truth, we will have a clearer understanding and acceptance of our Father's amazing love.

When we enter Father God's presence, His love and acceptance are openly extended to us and we can position ourselves at His feet. Choosing to remain there requires a daily commitment. Outside influences and self-gratification are constant enemies that attempt to drag us away from home. Like the prodigal son in our parable, we easily become dissatisfied with our life and leave home in search of a good time. We look to others for love, acceptance, and success. Media constantly bombards us with the message that we need a certain new toy for our pleasure or for someone's acceptance. The list is endless, but the message is always the same: we will be worth much more once we have whatever is being offered. Will you choose the immediate gratification offered by the world, or will you remain in your Father's presence? Personally, I want to be intently focused on my Father. If someone wants to tell me what a good guy I am, fine. But they will have to look over my Father's shoulder to find me. I'll accept their words and appreciate them, but I won't require them. I will already be basking in my Father God's loving acceptance.

Chapter 2: The Prodigal Son

I will have decided to find success and acceptance through Him, not the world.

The voices of the world will constantly attempt to call you away from your Father. Your self-worth will be attacked, and you will be "told" to do this or that to gain approval. Only when you follow those voices will you believe you are finally worthy of acceptance. If you fall for this, you will find yourself running in circles. Ultimately, you will drift farther and farther away from God until you are unable to hear His voice. You will discover you have left home and wonder how it happened. The remedy is simple. Run back to your Father. There you will receive His unconditional love and acceptance, something the world does not and cannot understand. Only at the feet of the Father will the voices of the world have no control over you. There you will realize your true value and discover how cherished you really are.

Making the choice to focus on the Father's voice may be obvious, but tuning out the noise of the world and listening to Him only is not an easy task. Once the decision is made to remain at Father God's feet and tune in to His voice, old habits that led you into trouble in the first place become well-laid traps to lure you away. Placed where least expected, stepping into them causes old behaviors to arise. At this point you must turn back to your Father God and rely on Him to give you the strength to escape. He will assist you without judgment.

One trap the enemy uses against me is my insecurity. When church visitors leave before I conclude my message, the old Insecurity Trap immediately snaps around my spiritual ankles. I jump to the conclusion I must have said something offensive, and now this visitor thinks I'm a real jerk. It does not matter that there's no basis for my thoughts. I believe them anyway. Next week: same trap, different bait. This time I may assume my message was a complete disaster. Why didn't I use this word instead of another one? Because I have allowed these thoughts to control my life, I find myself completely out of sorts. Ironically, as I torment myself about what others think of me, they aren't thinking about me at all.

Those who seek approval, acceptance, and success from the world live a conditional love life. Living this way is hard work, believe me. Cold-hearted and mean-spirited defense mechanisms develop around the heart to survive. Sadly, at that point you have left home and entered a foreign country. This new land appears beautiful, but danger lies below the surface. If only a warning sign would appear when we begin to look for approval and love from the world. I believe there is such a warning, and it comes in the person of the Spirit of God. Listen for His voice and He will sound a warning when you begin to wander down the wrong road. Take a moment now to examine your life. Where do you look for acceptance? Whose approval is important to you? Have you recently stepped into a trap that has led you to a foreign land?

Yeshua described the distant foreign country in the parable as a place where the son lost his sense. It was a place of insanity. After months or maybe even years of partying and living his worldly lifestyle, the son found himself in a pigpen ready to eat slop. He could have died in that pigpen if he hadn't come to his senses. Recognizing the depths to which he had fallen, he thought of his father and realized he was ready to go home. He hoped his father would receive him. Likewise, we can come to our senses, leave behind the insanity of seeking others' approval, turn to our Father God, and return home. Without question, He will lovingly receive us.

Speaking of love, it plays a large part in this parable. The first few times I read the story, I thought the father didn't have much love for his younger son. Understanding how dangerous the world can be, why did the father allow his son to leave? He could have said, "No, son. I know what is best for you. Stay here with your family." The son may have mumbled about how

CHAPTER 2: THE PRODIGAL SON

his father did not understand. He may have kicked rocks and complained to his older brother, but he would have gotten over it and stayed safely at home. If this had been the story line for the parable, it would have made for a short story. Yeshua wanted to make another point that was vitally important to His listeners then, as well as to those reading the parable today, a point that may affect your view of life if you listen for God to speak to you. It has everything to do with love and freedom.

This was exactly what the son was looking for: love and freedom. But the freedom he chose would begin with soft, velvet-covered claws. The son selfishly and rashly demanded his share of his future inheritance, intending to take it and run. Dad knew his son's heart and understood the dangers his son could encounter if he took out on his own. Living the party life does not lend itself to good decision-making. The rebellious son would learn that hard lesson on his own. The father loved his son enough to let him walk away and make his own mistakes. In his heart, he wanted the son he loved to stay home with him, but he realized that a forced love is not love at all. Yeshua wanted to emphasize this point.

When I met my wife over 40 years ago, I knew immediately she was the one for me. I thought, "Wow, I'm going to marry this girl, and she's not getting away." Right there I could have pulled a set of handcuffs out of my pocket, slapped them on her wrists and announced, "You are marrying me." I could have hauled her to a justice of the peace and forced her to marry me. Had I done so, what are the chances that Joan, standing before me in handcuffs, would have looked at me with starry eyes and said, "Oh, Marty, I love you more than I can say?" One hundred percent zero. Since Joan would have had no say in the matter, love could not have grown in our relationship.

God could have "slapped us in handcuffs" and dragged us off to His house and demanded we love Him. He could have programmed us to be robots that loved only Him. He could have created the angels to be His bride. But He did not do any of those things. Instead, He created Adam and Eve and placed them in a beautiful garden designed especially for their enjoyment. These two special people would have an intimate fellowship with God. He would love them, walk with them, talk with them, and together they would enjoy all of creation. True pleasure would come in the love they shared; a love freely given. God freely gave His love, but would Adam and Eve remain faithful in their love for Him? Of course, we know they did not. They chose to disobey God and turn their backs on Him.

The choice given to Adam and Eve continues to this day. You have the privilege of choosing to love your heavenly Father and walk with Him. When Yeshua returns for His bride He will say, "Of her own free will she chose Me. I did not force her. The devil did all he could to prevent her from following Me, but she chose Me." Because of love He created us, and because of that love, He has given us the choice to love Him.

The father in our parable allowed his son to make the choice to leave or stay home with his family. When we make the choice to "leave home," our Father God will always let us go. But He will await your return and continually watch for you. If your choice is to leave, you will have to choose whether you return or stay in the foreign land.

Having made his choice, the son left home and began his journey. His step may have had a jaunty bounce to it. The world was his to explore, and he was off to live the life he had always wanted. Fun, parties, and all kinds of adventures awaited him. It was exhilarating for a time, but his inheritance dwindled little by little until it was completely gone. To make matters worse, a famine spread through the country where the son had been living. Finding himself without means, the son hired himself out. He found a man willing to employ him, but his circumstances did not greatly improve. Before long he discovered the depths to which he had fallen. His employer sent him into the field to feed his animals. Not just any animals, but pigs. Cold reality hit him in the face. Party time was over. Out of money, he had no food, no friends, and no home. The jaunty bounce in his step was long gone. For the first time in his life, the young man was faced with utter desperation. His situation was so bad that he was ready to eat the slop he carried to the pigs.

Have you been in a similar situation, or are you now? If so, there is one simple—but tough—question to ask. "Who am I, really?" Before you answer, examine who you are at the very core of your being. Do not identify with your reputation, the money you make, or with how important you think you are. Your image is not the real you, but the stuff of conditional love land. Look past the image into your heart.

It should be obvious a comparison is being made for contrasting lifestyles. On one side there is an enticement of unrestricted opportunity for lavish living, ready acceptance by important people, and pleasure for the taking. This is the way of the world. On the other hand, there is a life that can be lived in the Father's love as Yeshua demonstrated. This is the Kingdom of God. While it may sound like a rigid and restrictive life, it brings great freedom.

When I stood in the dark alley I told you about earlier, I had to ask myself who I was. I could not provide an answer by looking at myself in the mirror. Instead, I had to shut down my ego and block out every image the world reflected to me. It took courage, and it was difficult. As I took a long, deep look into who I was I found a whole lot of smelly trash. God did not allow me to dwell in that garbage, though. In His love He showed me a beautiful truth. I was nothing more, and nothing less, than a child of Father God. I was a son of the living God. I knew beyond a doubt that I must return to Him. There I would find hope and be truly valued. I became filled with an all-encompassing peace as I began to understand who I really was.

I had come to my senses, making it possible to move forward in a new way.

It would not be long before the son in our parable faced his own moment of truth. As he fed the pigs, he considered how his lifestyle had led him to this place. Hungry and lonely, he began to consider his options. Earlier, he had avoided stability and security. Now they sounded more enticing by the minute. One day he looked up and said, "I am a son. I have a father!" He decided to return home and tell his father he had sinned against him. He was willing to humble himself to the point of becoming a servant, because he believed he was no longer worthy to be called his father's son. He just wanted to be home. Even though he was still in a distant country, hope sprang to life. In his heart, the journey home had already begun.

Hope always springs forth when you realize who you are as a child of God. It's absolutely freeing and acts as a buffer against the ugly bumps of life. The beautiful words, "My Father loves me," begins to roll through your mind, regardless of your situation. You may lose your job, but you can still walk down the street and sing like a bird because "my Father loves me." That same hope will accompany you as you travel from a distant country back to your home. Tell yourself you are a child of God as you return to Him with hope in your heart.

The son in our parable had a hopeful heart as he turned away from the pigs, walked out of the field, and began his long journey home. As he walked, he prepared himself to meet his father. He would have pondered how to approach his father and exactly which words he would speak. We all have had opportunities to rehearse similar lines. When I turned back to God, I remember thinking, "Well, when I give my life back to the Lord, maybe I can help with janitorial work somewhere. Perhaps after ten years of service, God will like me at least a little bit." The easy trap of conditional love springs up again. Perhaps you have said, "You know, Lord, I was tired and had a sore throat and didn't accomplish what I told you I would do. I'll do better next time. But may I still get a hug from You?" Or how about this: "You don't need to do anything for me today, Lord, because I know I don't deserve it." "I know, I know. You just put up with me. It's okay, though, because I know how rotten I am." You go through life rejecting the Father's love, maybe even pouting a little here and there. "I know I'm not blessed, God, but I'll be okay. You can bless someone else because they are better than I am. I'm used to it."

Why would the son believe he had to practice these lines? "I no longer deserve to be called your son, but if you let me be your servant, at least I'll have something to eat." "I know I'm your son, but I'm rotten. I would be happy to be one of your servants if I can have something to eat." Consider your own approach to God the next time you meet with Him. Listen to yourself. I'm willing to bet at least one of you will say something like this: "Well, God, here I am. Yeah, I yelled at the kids this morning and now You won't show up." "I haven't given any money at church lately, which means You won't bless me." I believe we talk like this because we don't really know our Father. The Bible tells us of God's love. Preachers have preached about it, teachers have taught it, and countless books have been written on the subject, yet we still struggle to accept God's unconditional love. Perhaps past abuse from a father-figure clouds our understanding of God's unconditional love, or it could be plain old ignorance. I don't know the reason behind the son's misunderstanding of his father's love, but at least he had the revelation that he was his father's son. He made the choice to go home and do whatever was necessary to "earn" his father's love again.

No effort is required to earn the love of our Father God. It isn't necessary to rehearse what you will say when you approach Him. Just turn and walk straight into His arms. He's standing at the property line, watching and waiting for you with unconditional love. When you recognize this truth and walk in it, you won't hesitate to talk with God about your frailties, backsliding, wrongdoings, and not-good-enough doings. You will look at your Father and fearlessly say, "Here I am."

This is what Yeshua wanted his listeners to comprehend. He knew they would focus on how the son was received by his father when he returned home. They would have expected Yeshua to say the son was severely beaten, maybe unto death. Instead, the father's unconditional love was on display. Through the example of the father in the parable, Yeshua showed His audience His Father's amazing love. He wanted them to understand that God does not want or need to hear excuses before He bestows love on His children. He doesn't expect a list of failures or any explanation of how you will make up for them. His only desire is to hear your voice speaking against His chest, "I'm home. I'm home."

I read a story in the "Faith" section of our newspaper that provides a beautiful illustration of a prodigal son's return. It was about Bill, a man who had struggled with alcoholism for years. He had been in many treatment centers, but every time he was released, he fell back into his old ways. In 1934, doctors told Bill's wife he was a hopeless drunk, and there was no hope for him apart from the grave. Later that same year, Bill entered a hospital for treatment of the DTs. An old friend visited him, and following a short conversation, he told Bill that his only hope of liberation lay in a religious conversion. As Bill lay in his hospital bed, he thought about what he had been told. He concluded he would never give up booze on his own, but stubbornly refused to ask God for help. After much soul-searching, Bill finally realized God was his only hope. He declared in desperation that he would do anything to be free from the grip of alcohol. He cried out to God, "Show Yourself, if You really exist!" To Bill's utter astonishment, his room became filled with a bright light.

Bill was smack in the middle of a pig pen in a distant country, totally unable to do anything to save himself. Death seemed to

CHAPTER 2: THE PRODIGAL SON

be the only way out. Bill sent out a heartfelt cry, "Daddy, if you're there, let me know." And He did. The power of God's Spirit instantly healed Bill, and he never touched another drop of alcohol. This hopeless drunk had found a Father who had been waiting for him to come home.

Now for the rest of the story. Bill went on to found Alcoholics Anonymous, an organization that has helped liberate millions from the trap of alcoholism. Through the 12-step program he initiated, Bill has provided a way for others to find their freedom.

We are children of our Father God. We should consider this revelation regularly as it will liberate us from much of the grief and strife we experience. It will deliver us from a religion that preaches we are not good enough for God, and that we should get our act together to become better people. Religion forces us to rehearse our lines, erect defenses, and desperately hope we won't be found guilty. Notice the son said, "I am your son; I'm just not worthy to be your son." We often live our lives focused on thoughts like these. "I am not worthy. I am not worthy." This is an easy trap to fall into because we are surrounded by messages that teach conditional love.

God's actions fly in the face of religion. He extends His hand to His child and says, "You are my beloved and I accept you and love you as you are." The son in the parable basically had wished his father dead, had wasted all the money he had been given, and smelled like a filthy pig. Not one person in the parable or any of Yeshua's listeners thought the son had any redeeming qualities. In their eyes, he was no good. In his father's eyes, he was fully acceptable upon his return.

This message was in Yeshua's parable, if only His listeners would hear it. He wanted them to know God the Father accepts His children unconditionally, just as the son in the parable was accepted. The parable is in our Bible to make us aware that we need to move from a land of conditional love into a land of unconditional love. It shows us we can say, "My daddy God still fully accepts me. I'm home. I have done very little right in my life, but despite my mistakes God accepts me as I am." The parable is simple, yet the message has a deep impact.

I have returned to various foreign lands frequently since the day I returned to my Father God. I have felt unworthy to pastor a church many times. Even though I knew better than to let these thoughts take root, I still wondered what others thought of me. If I didn't know what they were thinking, I'd think I knew. I played out in my mind every imaginable conversation I might encounter, and I always portrayed myself in a negative light. I believed I wasn't good enough to be a pastor. I told God at length how worthless I was, as if He didn't already know what I was thinking. I've been on numerous journeys, but I can say with great relief and happiness that I have always returned home to a loving welcome.

I recently read about a young girl who experienced an extraordinary homecoming. I don't recall her name so I will call her Sarah. Like so many teenagers, Sarah became tired of her parents' old-fashioned rules and expectations. She wanted the freedom to listen to her own music, wear short skirts, and generally live her own life. As far as she was concerned, her parents didn't know anything. After her 15th birthday, she decided she would be happier without them.

One day, after an exceptionally heated argument with her father, Sarah stormed out of her house. "I hate you!" she shouted as the door slammed behind her. She stomped down the sidewalk as her father sadly watched her leave. Sarah didn't have much money, but she was able to purchase a one-way ticket to Detroit. Upon her arrival, Sarah began to walk through the city and plan her course of action. It wasn't long before a nice-looking man in a fancy car pulled up beside her. The man rolled down his window, leaned over, and smiled at Sarah. "May I buy you lunch?" he asked. After a short deliberation, Sarah accepted the invitation. She enjoyed a delicious meal as she chatted with her host. When the man learned Sarah had just arrived in Detroit, he offered to provide a place for her to stay. She gladly accepted what she thought was a kind, generous offer, and she thanked him profusely for the motel room he provided. The man continued to stay in contact with Sarah, and before long he began offered pills to her. The pills made her feel wonderful, better than she had ever felt. This was the life, she thought. Sarah's rescuer stayed in contact with her, and eventually he taught her how to please men. Sarah was a minor, and that made her worth a lot of money to the man with the fancy car. But as far as Sarah was concerned, Detroit provided everything she had been searching for: freedom, comfort, and independence.

Life in Detroit was one grand adventure. Unfortunately, adventures come to an end. Sarah began to experience uncomfortable symptoms of a mysterious illness. She eventually became so ill she could no longer perform her favors, and her "boss" walked out of her life. Sick and with no one to care for her, Sarah wandered the cold, noisy, unfriendly streets of Detroit. She was back where she had started, alone. She searched for a place to sleep and finally settled on a metal grate outside a department store. Using an old piece of cardboard as a blanket, she curled up on the grate and settled in for the night.

One day turned into many. Sarah begged and scrounged for food as she walked the streets of Detroit. Each night she returned to her "home" where she tried to get comfortable enough to sleep. She felt worse every day as sickness consumed her. One night she awakened shivering violently. In her misery, she realized her circumstances were not going to improve. Suddenly, a childhood memory surfaced. It was spring and she was running with joyful abandon through her father's cherry orchard. Longing clutched at her heart, and she sobbed as she hugged her cardboard blanket close to her chest. Sarah was cold, destitute, and desperately longed for the safety of home.

The next morning Sarah began to search for a pay phone. Once she located one, she paced in front of it while she worked up the courage to punch in her old home number. In the handset she heard the phone ring until an answering machine picked up. Fearful of how her family might react when they heard her voice, Sarah hung up without leaving a message. She called several more times after that, but the answering machine always picked up. She decided to call one more time, this time leaving a message. With a shaky voice, Sarah said, "Daddy, it's me. I'm going to buy a bus ticket and come home. If you can forgive me, would you please meet me at the bus station? It's okay if you can't. I'll look for you, but if I don't see you, I'll stay on the bus and go on to Canada."

Sarah walked to the bus station. She was hopeful, but she also dreaded her return. She wondered if her parents had even heard her message. With the little bit of money she had, Sarah purchased a ticket. When the bus arrived, she climbed in and found a seat. For seven hours she sat, and for seven hours she rehearsed the words she would say to her father. As the bus drew closer to home, she noticed big fluffy snowflakes hitting the window. Soon a road sign announced her hometown was only 25 short miles ahead. With pounding heart and sweaty hands, Sarah wondered if anyone would meet her at the station.

The bus pulled into the depot. Air brakes hissed as it stopped, and the door opened with a soft thud. Passengers began to gather their belongings, but Sarah sat frozen to her seat. She was too afraid to look out the window or to step off the bus. Passengers quietly filed past her and exited the bus. To delay the inevitable, Sarah pulled a compact out of her purse and checked her makeup and hair. When she looked up, she found she was the only passenger still in the bus. She placed the compact in her purse, wiped her hands on her jeans, rose from her seat, and slowly walked down the aisle. Thoughts raced through her mind: no one will meet me; someone will be here and read the riot act to me; no one will recognize me. She didn't know what to expect.

Chapter 2: The Prodigal Son

Sarah could feel her heart beating fast and hard as she stepped off the bus. Slowly, cautiously, she made her way to the door of the terminal. How could she face her father? How could she not? What if he wasn't there? What if he was?

Sarah was completely unprepared for what awaited her on the other side of the door. First, she saw her brothers and sisters. And there were her aunts and uncles and cousins, even her grandparents. Every relative in town, all 40 of them, had gathered inside the depot. Wearing party hats and blowing party whistles, they were gathered around a big "Welcome Home" sign. It was loud, it was noisy, and it was wonderful. What a welcome home party!

Dumbfounded, Sarah stopped inside the door as she stared at her family and struggled with her emotions. She could not believe her eyes. Her father slowly stepped out of the crowd and walked toward her. Taking a deep breath, Sarah began her prepared speech. "Daddy, I'm sorry for what I've done." Her father replied, "Hush, child," wrapped her in his big comforting arms, and held her close. "We're going to have a party," he said. "We've been waiting a long time for you to come home."

Sarah had returned to her father as a child, just as the son in the parable had returned. We must do the same. Yeshua said, "Unless you become like little children, you will not enter the kingdom of heaven" (Matthew 18:3). He didn't tell us to *remain* as children, but our approach is to be childlike. Accept His unconditional love, just as a child accepts his daddy's love. Trust Him completely. Let Him wrap His arms around you. Once you are home, with the help of the Holy Spirit, you can begin the process of being transformed into Yeshua's image.

A child safely held in the arms of his father experiences no fear. He doesn't wonder if someone is thinking badly of him. He doesn't fear he will be dropped or abandoned. He simply trusts his daddy. He experiences peace, happiness, contentment, and fulfillment. As a child of Father God, you can have the same experience. Keep your eyes on Him and you won't be concerned with what others think of you. You will know you are a child of your Father God. Return to the simplicity and innocence of what God desires. Even though you have a sinful human nature, you have been made perfect in Messiah. Enter His kingdom. Rest in His trustworthy arms.

Countless believers in Yeshua have found this rest. Imagine what it would look like if every one of them crowded together at the feet of God. Stretching for miles in every direction, God would look over the glorious sight with love in His eyes and reach out to embrace every person simultaneously. Each of His children would revel in His embrace and fully accept His love, unconcerned about what the person 60 miles distant was thinking. No one would wonder if he was good enough to be in God's presence. What a beautiful place to dwell. Hold this image close. When a religious spirit tries to convince you of how worthless you are, shrug off the condemnation and run into your Father's loving embrace.

While child-like faith and trust are critical, there is another important principle to consider. Yeshua told the Pharisee Nicodemus that no one can see the kingdom of God unless he is born again (John 3). Yeshua's statement deeply puzzled Nicodemus. There are several born-again experiences in Judaism, and Nicodemus had experienced all of them. Confused, Nicodemus asked Yeshua if he was to start over (enter his mother's womb) as that was the first born-again experience for a Jew. But Yeshua was telling Nicodemus that there was one more born-again experience, that of being born of the Spirit. Nicodemus had advanced through every born-again experience available to him and, except for his birth, had earned them all on his own merit. Being born of the Spirit was beyond human effort. By faith Nicodemus would have to be born again into the arms of the Father and find rest in His presence. "Nicodemus, teacher of Israel, you need to be born from above."

Likewise, we must be born of the Spirit. If you have not had this experience, ask God to be your daddy, to be your savior. It doesn't matter if you are in an ugly relationship, a hard situation, or if you have made horrible decisions in the past. Your Father God will receive you with open arms and say, "Welcome home." This is the Father God that Yeshua wanted His listeners to know.

My biological father died when I was very young so I never knew him. As a result, my perception of fatherhood and how to relate to a father has been hindered. Perhaps you have had a similar experience, or maybe you had an abusive father. Whatever your situation, ask God to help you step away from past hurtful experiences and to help you pursue Him. Seize the revelation that you are His child. He is a good Father, a Father of love, and His desire is for you to experience His acceptance and love in great measure.

So far, we envisioned the younger son in our parable as one coming home to God for the first time, a picture of salvation. We also approached him as a back-sliding believer who followed other gods, later returning from the foreign land he had entered. Moving forward we will observe the younger lost son as a representation of Yeshua HaMashiach.

Obviously, Yeshua was never lost. But like the younger son in our parable, He did leave His home and travel to a distant country. He walked a difficult path. There were many who didn't welcome Him. He was called a drunkard, a glutton, a friend of the hated tax collectors, and accused of blaspheming Almighty God. Despite the turmoil that surrounded Him, He consistently demonstrated and taught others how to approach His heavenly Father. He realized that He was in an unfriendly country, but He persevered through every hardship. At one point near the end of His earthly life, He pleaded with His Father to "take this cup from me" if possible. (See Mark 14:32–41.) Still, He remained determined to carry out His Father's will. Despised, tortured, and abandoned even by His best friends, Yeshua endured and chose obedience to His Father. When He hung on the execution stake, He bore all mankind's sin, the ultimate separation from His Father. After lying in the grave for three days, He rose from the dead and returned to His Father. Mission accomplished. He had successfully made the way for every man, woman, and child to approach Father God and be with Him forever. He endured torture, crucifixion, and descent into hell, all for the joy set before Him (Hebrews 12:2), the joy of returning home and reuniting with His Father. Yeshua, the obedient Son, would now present all who trusted in Him to His Father, calling those believers fellow sons and daughters of God.

> What I am saying is that as long as an heir is underage, he is no different from a slave, although he owns the whole estate. The heir is subject to guardians and trustees until the time set by his father. So also, when we were underage, we were in slavery under the elemental spiritual forces of the world. But when the set time had fully come, God sent his Son, born of a woman, born under the law, to redeem those under the law, that we might receive adoption to sonship. Because you are his sons, God sent the Spirit of his Son into our hearts, the Spirit who calls out, *"Abba,* Father." So you are no longer a slave, but God's child; and since you are his child, God has made you also an heir.
> —Galatians 4:1–7

This is a remarkable passage. When the time had fully come, God sent His son, born of a woman, born under the law, to redeem those under the law. This was accomplished to make the way for us to be adopted as sons of God. Not only would we be adopted as sons, but we would also receive the full rights of sonship. Because you are His son, God sent the Spirit of His Son into your heart. It's this Spirit in us who calls out, "Abba, Father." The Greek word for "call out" is *krazo,* which means "to exclaim or to cry out loudly." When we realize we are truly His child, and when the Spirit comes to dwell within us, we shout, "Abba, Father!" "Daddy!" We don't whisper the words as

Chapter 2: The Prodigal Son

if they are an embarrassment. Rather, it becomes impossible to remain quiet because we have a spiritual, supernatural, heavenly Father who is glorious beyond description, and He dwells in us.

As children of God, we no longer endure being enslaved to the world. This alone is glorious and fantastic, but there is more. We have also been made His heirs. Not only are we children of God, but He wants to give us the farm and a new tractor. Talk about the Father lavishing His love on us!

> For those who are led by the Spirit of God are the children of God. The Spirit you received does not make you slaves, so that you live in fear again; rather, the Spirit you received brought about your adoption to sonship. And by him we cry, "Abba, Father." The Spirit himself testifies with our spirit that we are God's children. Now if we are children, then we are heirs—heirs of God and co-heirs with Christ. . .
> —Romans 8:14–17a

The first letter of "Spirit" is capitalized in the passage above, indicating the Spirit is the person of God the Father. The Spirit Himself testifies with our spirit that we are God's children. If anyone doubts who he is in Yeshua, these verses make it crystal clear that we are His.

Returning to our parable, the father's son has returned and a celebration in his honor has been organized. This presents another angle from which we can approach our study. Many guests would have been invited and there would have been an abundance of food. Not just any food, but the very best would have been laid out to celebrate this joyous occasion. There would have been live music, and guests would have danced the evening away. It would have been a very exciting night. We can view this celebration and feast like the one we are invited to when the church is caught up to be with God. Now *that* will be a party! I believe it will be much like the Feast of Sukkot (Tabernacles) celebration, the annual feast designed to remind the Israelites that God was their Great Shepherd and that He chose to "tabernacle (live) among them." It also sounds remarkably like the Spirit being sent to dwell in us. Ultimately, the 1,000-year celebration planned for us will be on a much grander scale than what the father provided for his prodigal son.

We have covered exhaustively the story of the younger son in our parable. For the most part, his role has been easy to understand. We turn now to the older brother's situation, where we will encounter several challenges.

When I began to look at big brother's story, I found myself reluctant to dig too deeply into my study. I finally asked God to reveal to me the source of my hesitation, and He showed me that I was hesitant to remain a participant in the story. I felt uncomfortable and wanted to back away. The first part of the parable contained wonderful truths that felt good. They blessed me. What I saw in the older son was abrasive and made me uneasy. It would be much easier to step back into the role of an observer and simply watch how events played out.

Still hesitant, I began to probe the older brother's situation. As I proceeded, I made a conscious effort to step out of the Observer role, leave the younger son at his party, and participate in this new situation. Much to my surprise, I found more healing and blessing in these passages than I had experienced with the younger son. I invite you to open your heart to this new role and discover the same.

> "Meanwhile, the older son was in the field. When he came near the house, he heard music and dancing. So he called one of the servants and asked him what was going on. 'Your brother has come,' he replied, 'and your father has killed the fattened calf because he has him back safe and sound.' The older brother became angry and refused to go in. So his father went out and pleaded with him. But he answered his father, 'Look! All these years I've been slaving for you and never disobeyed your orders. Yet you never gave me even a young goat so I could celebrate with my friends. But when this son of yours who

has squandered your property with prostitutes comes home, you kill the fattened calf for him!' 'My son,' the father said, 'you are always with me, and everything I have is yours. But we had to celebrate and be glad, because this brother of yours was dead and is alive again; he was lost and is found.'"

—Luke 15:25–31

At first glance, it is apparent the older son was lost. He had a bad attitude, and if he desired any healing at all, he would have to overcome it. As we proceed, we will discover that his situation was very complex. He had worked hard in the field the day his brother returned. This wasn't anything out of the ordinary. What was unusual was the music and revelry he heard as he approached the house. He called out to a nearby servant and asked what was taking place. He could have run into the house and joined the festivities. "Alright! Party! I'll clean up and join you. Be sure to save me some food!" Or he could have run to his father and asked him what was going on. Both scenarios would have made a great parable. Everyone would have been blessed and very satisfied. But once again, Yeshua's deeper lesson would have been lost.

The servant explained to the older son that his brother had returned, and his father had ordered the fatted calf killed for a big celebration. The son stopped in his tracks. A party? For his no-good brother? Stunned, the older son became offended and angry, an attitude that robbed him of the joy he could have experienced. His anger came from a judgmental, condemning, self-righteous attitude rooted in unforgiveness, bitterness, and jealousy. Holding on to those attitudes, the older brother compared himself to his younger sibling. In the end, the older brother concluded he was the better man. This created a big problem. His attitude rendered him incapable of entering his own home to participate in a family celebration. To put it bluntly, he was unable to experience joy *when someone else received a blessing.*

This realization hit me like a ton of bricks. The Holy Spirit began to read my mail and brought to my remembrance incidents where I had reacted the same way. Talk about catching my attention! I realized I must constantly be aware of my attitude. With that in mind, I devised a test to check myself for negative reactions. It was a simple test. I would observe other people as they were blessed and judge how I responded. I found my reactions weren't always godly. I asked God to help me change, and then I leaned into the Holy Spirit for guidance. I began to ask people who attended other churches what God was doing in their fellowship. When I heard a wonderful report, I would reply, "Wow! That's great!" To be truthful, I was less interested in what God was doing for them than I was in my reaction to what they were receiving. As God blessed them, I wanted to be joyful. I determined that I would not become resentful if I didn't receive the same blessing. For years I had focused on my own and my church's blessings without giving much thought to how others were being blessed. In the middle of my self-imposed experiment, another realization hit me. I was lost just like the older son in the parable. I was every bit as messed up as he was. This realization caused me no small amount of mental anguish.

Unable to share in his father's joy, the older son angrily said to his father, "Look! All these years I have slaved for you and never disobeyed your orders, yet you never once gave me even a young goat for a celebration with my friends." Frustrated and bitter, he was completely focused on his own situation. He probably could have told anyone who asked exactly how long his brother had been gone and how much extra work fell to him as a result. The older son was convinced beyond a doubt that he was the better person by far. Blind to the reality of his situation, this brother had fallen into the trap of serving his father out of duty rather than serving in love.

Serving someone outside a love relationship is a form of slavery. I have watched this phenomenon occur in churches for years. An on-fire believer starts a ministry of service with zeal to spare, but as months and even years pass the believer slowly becomes less zealous and more mechanical. Feelings of being under-appreciated and over-worked gradually creep in. I'm sure you have either experienced this or witnessed it. The solution in this situation is to refocus on God and His love.

Each son in our parable experienced a form of slavery, but they differed greatly in how they saw themselves. The younger son left home seeking freedom, happiness, and a good time. Everything he desired may have been all about the flesh, but at least he knew what he wanted and went after it. Through a series of twists in the road he eventually found himself completely lost in a distant country. When he hit rock bottom, he realized how lost he was and decided to return home to his father.

On the other hand, the elder son didn't chase his dream or find contentment in his situation. Instead, he became the responsible son, the obedient son who stayed home and did everything expected of him. You may know this guy. He's the one who never has a problem with his flesh. He has never been drunk or indulged in drugs. He always smiles, never gets upset, and is a gracious servant. He's an all-around great guy. These characteristics could easily apply to the older son in the parable, but his façade concealed the real issue. The true state of his heart was revealed when his younger brother returned. Bitter feelings rose to the surface, and he lashed out at his father. Are you aware of the state of your heart? Yeshua wanted his listeners to look deep inside their hearts and discover who they really were. It's the only way to identify the real issue, the only way to make it possible for the Holy Spirit to do His healing work in each person.

This powerful message must be handled with care. Like me, you could probably make a list of people who need to hear it. These are dangerous thoughts, and they usually arise when you don't participate in the parable. Work with the Holy Spirit as He heals your heart, and let the Spirit work on the other person. We all need to hear this. Healing cannot come if it is ignored. In general, the church is paralyzed by not receiving this healing. If you've been in a church community for any length of time, you have seen this religious spirit at work time and again. Many have suffered from it or will experience it sometime in the future.

The first section of our parable had a wonderful, exciting ending. The younger son returned, his father accepted him, and a celebration followed. It's like the end of a feel-good movie where beautiful music plays as the main characters walk through a flower-filled meadow into the sunset. The section concerning the older son does not have a happy ending. There's no beautiful music, nor is there a lush meadow. Read the parable again and notice that Yeshua never finished the story of the older son. This son doesn't say, "Oh, father, I'm sorry. Let's go in and party. I want to hug my brother." I hope he eventually did say those or similar words, but Yeshua left it open-ended. As I studied the parable and realized what Yeshua had presented, I became frustrated. "You can't leave this guy hanging out there with no resolution," I thought. When I looked at it logically, however, I realized there had to be a reason for this lack of closure. After much prayer and meditation, I concluded the reason is as relevant today as when Yeshua told the parable.

There was only one way the older son could be healed. He had to realize he was lost. His next step would have been to go to his father and meet with him face to face. The same applies to each one of us as we seek to be healed. First, recognize there is something wrong with our heart. Second, enter our Father God's presence and meet with Him face to face. Without that humble attitude, healing will remain out of reach. The older son showed the father he had a heart problem, but I don't believe he understood how serious it was. Did he take the next step to hear his father's voice? In Luke 15:31 we read, "'My son,' the father said, 'you are always with me, and everything I have is yours." Notice the father said, "My son." Oh, the depth of the father's love! If the older son had recognized his desperate need and tuned in to his father's words, healing would have begun that very moment.

"My son," the father had said. Sadly, the son could not utter the answering word, "Father." To recognize you are a child of the Father and to speak His name is a critical step in the healing process. The older son missed it. Don't make the same mistake. When you approach your Father God with the attitude of a small child, the incredible response you will hear is, "My son (or daughter), everything I have is yours and I am with you always." Step into His arms and let your healing begin.

Each son in our parable would experience healing in different ways. The younger son had severed his relationship with his father when he left home. Upon his return, he received instant healing from his father. He was welcomed home and all was forgiven. The older son had remained with his father, but their relationship was far from intimate. Walls of anger and bitterness had been erected in this son's heart. He needed to approach his father, ask forgiveness for having a hard heart, and begin to renew their relationship. Unless he took those steps, he would remain lost and would not be healed. The older son had fallen into the "service trap" and performed his duties without genuine intimacy with his father. Yes, he was with his father each day, but their relationship was skewed. It was more a side-by-side relationship than it was relational.

The parable doesn't tell us if the older son took any steps to receive healing. His story doesn't have a resolution. Yeshua revealed the older son's character and left him standing outside the house. It is left to the listener to ponder what happened next.

If you have remained an observer as we've studied this parable, you probably created your own happy ending for the older son. But if you are an active participant, I hope you are examining your current relationship with God. Perhaps you have drifted away from intimacy with your Father and now perform good works out of duty. Maybe you strive to make up for someone else's lack of effort. If that is the case, dryness will eventually permeate your life of service. Bitterness and resentment will begin to creep in, and a sense of entitlement will seep into your thoughts. This is a serious, contagious, and cancerous condition. When you step away from an intimate relationship with the Father, even for a short time, the "works disease" will spring up and take over your life. Ministry is effective only when motivated by an intimate relationship with your Father God. Works undertaken on this basis will bring life and God's blessing to the ministry.

The older son had become focused on his work to the point that he lost sight of who he was. Without realizing it, he had let anger, bitterness, and jealousy spread into every area of his life. If he remained blind to the state of his heart, there is a very real possibility he remained lost for the rest of his life.

Likewise, many believers have become enslaved to anger and bitterness without realizing it. They are discouraged, tired, offended, dry to the bone, self-righteous, and judgmental. When they finally understand their attitude, they believe it can be fixed by performing acceptable acts of service. Without the intimacy of their Father God, however, their work will be without God's anointing. All works motivated by selfishness result in an attitude of self-righteousness. "I do more than so-and-so, and I do it better." Jealousy rears its ugly head. "I've been in ministry longer than Joe Smith and I've worked harder. Why does his ministry grow while mine doesn't?" "We struggle to hold on to our little church building while the church down the street has a new million-dollar building. We deserve a new church more than they do."

Becoming consumed with these thoughts makes it impossible to be joyful when someone else is blessed. I want to be joyful when someone experiences God's blessing. I don't want to stand outside the house with an angry and resentful attitude while others enter and experience God's blessing. When those emotions

Chapter 2: The Prodigal Son

arise, I have determined to cry out to my Abba Father, "Lord, help me! I'm the lost older son standing outside your door, and I want to enter and be with You." Reach out to Father God, touch Him, and listen as He says, "My son" or "My daughter." Enter His presence and let His mercy and grace flow over you. You will discover your worst enemy can no longer intimidate you since you have been filled with God's love and peace. Remain in His house and develop the intimate love relationship your Father God desires to share with you.

Individuals in a close relationship reveal their level of intimacy in the way they speak to each other. It is obvious when they are deeply bonded. It is just as obvious when they are not. The first words spoken by the older son to his father in our parable revealed the nature of their relationship. Words of complaint poured out of the son's mouth. "Look, all these years I've been slaving for you and never disobeyed your orders." "All these years," he said. He had worked long and hard for his father, but his work had been largely invested in farm duties at the expense of family relationship. His words exposed a lack of intimacy. Someone who hasn't known the Lord very long may think this son wasn't very smart, which may be the case. But be very careful. You may fall into the same trap one day. These traps are set in such a way that you don't realize you have walked into them until it's too late. Remain alert. The longer you serve the Lord, the easier it is to become a victim. How I wish this weren't the case, but Yeshua shared the parable because it does occur. Continue to do your works of service, but do them with God's anointing.

The issue with the older son was not one of service to his father. It was a heart problem. A believer is on fire when he first receives Yeshua as savior, then over time, his heart begins to lose some of that fire. He turns inward and becomes self-centered. "Don't you get it, God? I have served you all these years and what do I get?" The trap is set. The joy in their life is less spontaneous. The intimate relationship with God that once brought delight occurs less and less often. Slowly the trap closes.

They engage in good works to fill the empty place inside them, believing this activity will restore their relationship with God. "Serve harder, serve longer, and the joy will come back." Some may say, "I just need to increase my service and hope the Lord will be happy with me. If I'm successful, He'll bless me and show everyone what I've done." Paradoxically, this self-centered attitude separates them from the Father. The trap closes tighter. They become filled with bitterness, jealousy, criticism, and judgment. Complaints begin to pour out of their mouths. They're still doing good works, but as God's anointing disappears, their intimate relationship with God is gone. It's critical that they come to their senses, or they will become bone-dry spiritually.

Unfortunately, I have been one of those burned-out believers, and that is why I found it difficult to participate in the older son role. Truth was staring me in the face, and I didn't want to deal with it. I struggled as I studied, wrote, prayed, meditated, and rewrote. In the end I felt as though I'd been hit over the head with a two-by-four. I feel three inches shorter than I was only a few weeks ago.

Slowing down, I was able to consider my journey into performing good works out of a sense of duty. God wanted me to do some soul-searching before I continued my study. You see, when I first returned to God, I was ecstatic that He would even notice me, let alone allow me to serve Him. I was so happy, I wanted to jump with joy. I even went to Resurrection Fellowship's construction site as they built their new church and made myself available to help in any capacity. As I worked, I would ask myself, "Don't these people know how simple I am? Why do they let me help with this building? I'm not even worthy to pick up a hammer. When will God tell them what I'm really like?" I fully expected someone to discover the truth about me and kick me off the property. That didn't happen, though, and I gradually allowed myself to relax. "Wow, God likes me! He's letting me serve Him." It was as if He had no memory. "Oh, thank you,

CHAPTER 2: THE PRODIGAL SON

God. I appreciate what You are doing." I felt deeply honored as tears filled my eyes.

It grieves me to say that my exuberance didn't last. Later, although the thoughts I entertained were different, I still had a heart problem. "After all these years, why don't I get more recognition?" "Why do others receive more blessings than I experience?" "Why can't we have a bigger place to worship and a better dance floor?" As those attitudes and many more grew, the spontaneous joy I used to have faded away. Where was the happy person who used to enter the presence of God with such jubilation? Where was the man who thrived on serving Him? I was resentful of those who seemed to be exceedingly blessed. I wasn't getting what I deserved. I wanted more recognition. Unknowingly, I had become enslaved to my own self-centeredness. How had I gone from, "You mean I can come in?" to "I don't see why I'm not blessed like the guy over there!" The answer is that I had let the self-centered "after all these years" attitude re-enter my heart. God had placed me in a situation where my heart condition was laid bare before me. How I handled this realization was now up to me.

The older son did not seem to recognize his situation. He seemed to throw caution to the wind as he bitterly continued his complaints. "This son of yours has squandered your property with prostitutes." Angry words spilled out of his mouth. If we watched this scene in a movie, we might cheer the son and agree that he had good reason to be upset. His no-good bum of a brother had wasted his inheritance and spent time with prostitutes, and now he had the nerve to return. Adding insult to injury, dad killed the fatted calf to celebrate his rotten brother's return. He was extremely offended, unaware that the true condition of his heart had been exposed. Unfortunately, the older son remained blind to his own shortcomings.

The older son continued his rant, but his father did not address a single complaint. He simply looked his son in the eye and said, "My son, you are always with me, and everything I have is yours." He didn't compare the sons or tell the older one he was the better person. The father's heart held the same love for both, and love drove the father outside to plead with his older son to join the party. "Look around you," his father said. "All I have is yours." He went straight to the heart of the matter.

The older son could have had the desire of his heart at that very moment. When his father invited him to join the party, he should have said, "Yes, Father." He should have expressed joy at his brother's return and joined the festivities. He would have received healing and his story would have had a happy ending, but because he had hardened his heart it wasn't going to be that easy.

It takes time to soften a hardened heart. It takes a lot of effort and significant assistance from the Holy Spirit. It is difficult to change attitudes when a heart is filled with bitterness, hurt, and unforgiveness. Thick walls that have been erected around the heart are not easily torn down, especially when defense mechanisms are locked firmly in place. If only it could be as simple as saying, "What a good idea. I'll just change my heart and enter my Father's house." But the hard-hearted person must let go of those bad attitudes and pray for the grace to get through the process. He must invite God's Spirit to guide him into an intimate relationship with Father God, a relationship of paramount importance. God alone will change the heart.

A strategy I've used in my own healing process may prove helpful. Earlier I explained how I approached others to discover how God was blessing them. I would gauge my reaction, and if I found myself angry with someone or struggling to forgive them, I would pick up my checkbook and send an offering to them. Offerings are a useful tool. "Take that, devil. Don't try to pull me down with the old unforgiveness trick." Try it. Engage in spiritual warfare for your own sake and set yourself free. I can already hear a voice in the back of the room. "But pastor, you don't know what they did to me." Don't get too close to me when you speak those words. I may tell you to send a bigger offering. Throw self-pity out the door. It's a trap straight from the pit of hell.

If you find yourself complaining like the older son in our parable, ask the Holy Spirit to help you clean up your vocabulary. Be aware of the words you speak, and avoid chronic complainers. Find new friends if necessary. Evaluate the state of your heart, and allow the Spirit of God to reveal where you stand.

As God heals your heart you will experience God's presence in a new way and your joy will increase. He will tell you all He has is yours. You will hear Him say He will never leave you. Any complaints you may have had will become insignificant, and reverence for your Father God will expand deep in your soul. This, my friend, is the servant's heart. I could write a long chapter just on this subject, but for now consider this reverential aspect. The blood of Yeshua has enabled you to enter the presence of Almighty God. You don't "get to" serve Him because you are smart or because you have earned the right. It is only by God's grace that you serve the King. The true servant's heart appreciates the privilege of serving and will do so with thankfulness and reverence.

The points Yeshua made in the context of the prodigal son are also found in other parables. The Parable of the Pharisee and the Tax Collector is one example.

To some who were confident of their own righteousness and looked down on everyone else, Jesus told this parable:

> "Two men went up to the temple to pray, one a Pharisee and the other a tax collector. The Pharisee stood by himself and prayed: 'God, I thank you that I am not like other people—robbers, evildoers, adulterers—or even like this tax collector. I fast twice a week and give a tenth of all I get.' But the tax collector stood at a distance. He would not even look up to heaven, but beat his breast

and said, 'God, have mercy on me, a sinner.' I tell you that this man, rather than the other, went home justified before God. For all those who exalt themselves will be humbled, and those who humble themselves will be exalted."

—Luke 18:9–14

This scene, which included a righteous Pharisee and a repentant tax collector, was easy to identify with. The Pharisee engaged in the comparison game, just as the older son did in our first parable. In this parable, the man who humbled himself would receive God's mercy and be justified before Him, but the man who exalted himself would be humbled by God. I have been in the latter position too many times. It was never a pleasant experience, but God in His wisdom and love knew I needed to learn a lesson. Better to be humbled by God than to remain in a self-exalted position.

A similar lesson appears in The Parable of the Unmerciful Servant.

Then Peter came to Jesus and asked, "Lord, how many times shall I forgive my brother or sister who sins against me? Up to seven times?" Jesus answered, "I tell you, not seven times, but seventy-seven times. Therefore, the kingdom of heaven is like a king who wanted to settle accounts with his servants. As he began the settlement, a man who owed him ten thousand bags of gold was brought to him. Since he was not able to pay, the master ordered that he and his wife and his children and all that he had be sold to repay the debt. At this, the servant fell on his knees before him. 'Be patient with me,' he begged, 'and I will pay back everything.' The servant's master took pity on him, canceled the debt and let him go. But when that servant went out, he found one of his fellow servants who owed him a hundred silver coins. He grabbed him and began to choke him. 'Pay back what you owe me!' he demanded. "His fellow servant fell to his knees and begged him, 'Be patient with me, and I will pay it back.' But he refused. Instead, he went off and had the man

CHAPTER 2: THE PRODIGAL SON

thrown into prison until he could pay the debt. When the other servants saw what had happened, they were outraged and went and told their master everything that had happened. Then the master called the servant in. 'You wicked servant,' he said, 'I canceled all that debt of yours because you begged me to. Shouldn't you have had mercy on your fellow servant just as I had on you?' In anger his master handed him over to the jailers to be tortured, until he should pay back all he owed. This is how my heavenly Father will treat each of you unless you forgive your brother or sister from your heart."
—Matthew 18:21–35

The servant owed the king 10,000 bags of gold or, as the Greek text states, ten thousand talents. In Yeshua's day one talent was worth approximately 20 years of a day-laborer's wages. Think how much this man owed! No servant would be able to repay such a debt. The King knew this, which led him to order the man, along with his family and possessions, be sold to recoup his loss. This was a terrible blow to the servant, and he pleaded for mercy. Incredibly, his master extended mercy and graciously forgave the debt.

The servant, free of his obligation to the king, should have been filled with joy and relief. Maybe he was for a brief time, but deep inside he was suffering from a serious malady. After he left the presence of his master, he found a fellow servant who owed him 100 coins. The Greek text states the amount was one hundred denarii, or four months' wages for a day laborer. (In Jesus' day, a daily wage was one denarius. See Matthew 20:2.) Putting things into perspective, this was roughly 1/100th of the amount the servant had owed the king. Just as the first servant had pleaded with the king, this servant pleaded for mercy and said he would repay the debt. Blinded to how this situation duplicated his own earlier plight, the first servant became enraged and grabbed the other servant's throat. In his fury he shouted, "You dirty bum! Give me my money or I'm going to kill you!" (My paraphrase.) In due course, the first servant was ordered to appear before the King. Because this servant had been granted mercy, he should have extended mercy and forgiveness to the man who owed him money. The King handed the servant over to the jailers and ordered them to torture him until he could repay his entire debt.

The point of this parable is forgiveness. To walk in God's blessing, you must be a person who forgives. Practice forgiveness and you will experience God's blessings many times over. Your life will radically change when you release personal offense and choose forgiveness. Ultimately, you will discover that the more you forgive, the more you will seek opportunities to forgive.

The king in this parable represents our Father God who has forgiven every one of us through Yeshua HaMashiach. The ultimate in mercy and forgiveness has been extended to us. What we do with His gift is up to us. We can choose to ignore it, or we can choose to extend it to others. If we ignore it and continue to hold unforgiveness in our hearts, the parable above tells us God will turn us over to the tormentor. A prime example of this is King Saul. He had killed thousands, but became jealous when songs were written about David killing tens of thousands. He developed feelings of inferiority, much as the older son in our first parable. Saul became afflicted with a tormenting spirit and soon became enraged. In the unmerciful servant parable, Yeshua said the same thing would happen to anyone who did not extend forgiveness and mercy to others. You cannot become jealous and filled with unforgiveness to the point you want to choke those who mistreat you. Forgive, and humbly approach your heavenly Father where you will discover healing and freedom. His arms are open, and He waits to surround you with His love.

The father in The Parable of the Lost Son surrounded both of his sons with love. We know this because his open arms were extended to each one. He never compared one son to the other. He could have said to the older, "Yeah, your brother was pretty messed up, I know. You're right. But cut him a little slack; he's just a punk kid." Instead, the father maintained an even temperament. As I read the older son's complaints, I have wondered why his father didn't bless him with his own party. If he loved his sons equally, why not treat them equally?

Yeshua always chose precise words to make His point, so there must be an explanation for how this parable was presented. I just didn't know what it was. Continuing my study and meditation I eventually received an answer from the Holy Spirit. It brought healing to me, and I hope it will to you as well. God showed me that each of His children is unique. Just as each son in the parable was unique, God created each of us with a specific purpose in mind. We all have God-given talents and personalities. We all have our likes and dislikes. God is in the process of building a house that has many different living stones. He loves every unique stone (person) in a special way, and His expression of love is tailored specifically for each person.

The father in The Parable of the Lost Son expressed love for his younger son with open arms, a big embrace, and a welcome-home party. Their relationship had been restored. The father's relationship with his older son, however, was not close. Desiring more intimacy, the father went outside and asked him to come into the house where he could celebrate his brother's return. It was here that God showed me why the father hadn't provided a party for his older son. The father realized this son never really wanted one, regardless of what he had told his father. The younger son was the party animal, not the older son. The father would express love toward his older son in a manner more appropriate to that son's personality. He loved both of his sons just as they were, and that love drove the father outside the house to invite his older son to come back with him and participate in the celebration. Such is God's great love for us that He will come outside to invite us into His house. He doesn't ask us to change our behavior or attitudes before He approaches us. He loves us where we are. The father in the parable loved his older son just as he was. It was a beautiful picture of Father God's love.

God expresses His love to each one of us based on who we are. God may respond to a believing NFL player with a high five, but to a little girl who wouldn't hurt a flea He may extend a little hug and kiss on the cheek. Imagine what it would look like if God reversed those expressions. The big NFL player would be much more excited to receive the high five than a little hug and kiss, and the little girl would be overwhelmed if God gave her a big smacking high five. The *expression* of God's love varies from person to person.

I have a huge sense of adventure. I live for it. I need it and even require it in my life. Knowing this, God demonstrates His love for me in adventurous ways. His expressions of love toward me include scenery with big vistas. In some instances, His expression of love is like a volcano, or even a tornado. Other times His love is expressed through beautiful songs or symphonic-style music, majestic mountains, or rushing rivers. His love for me is exhibited in many ways, but it always says, "Marty, I love you!"

I experienced a mighty river of God's love in an adventure that took place in the Rocky Mountains. I frequently camp in the mountains because I find it beautiful and relaxing. After one camping trip, I drove home through the Poudre Canyon and was struck by the beauty of God's creation. I pulled over so I could immerse myself in the sound of the river's rushing water, the colors of nature, and the rustle of wind through the leaves. Standing on the bank of the Poudre River, I struck up a conversation with God. As I enjoyed the fellowship and the scenery, I turned and looked upstream where an unbelievable sight unfolded. Three young men were riding the river, not on a boat or wooden raft, but on an air mattress. On top of that, they were quickly approaching a stretch of rapids. I can't begin to tell you how excited I became. These adventurous men were having the time of their lives. My only hope was that they wouldn't crash on the rocks as I really didn't want to get in the cold, fast-moving mountain

Chapter 2: The Prodigal Son

water to rescue them. On the other hand, I certainly didn't mind living this adventure through them.

I figured they had at least some common sense because they were wearing helmets, so I wasn't overly concerned for their safety. As I watched the spectacle, I noticed the men were under water almost as often as they were above it. The air mattress bounced through the rapids and slid through the rocks. I couldn't stop a big smile from spreading across my face. As I mentally cheered the group on, I decided this was great entertainment. Suddenly, one of the men fell into the cold, fast-moving water. I watched as he swished by in front of me, the current carrying him down the river. When he spied a big rock, he made his way over to it and climbed to safety. He had scraped his hands and knees, but at least he was safe. The man sat on the rock and watched as his two buddies floated down the river without him. While the men on the air mattress laughed and shouted exuberantly, the one sitting on the rock was not having a good time. He had been forced out of the river and left high and dry on a rock.

Well, maybe not so dry. Because the water was freezing, I knew he was as well. His hands and knees were probably stinging, and the rock he sat on was far from comfortable. He had a decision to make. He looked at his friends who were getting farther and farther away. He turned his head and looked at me. He finally began to work his way around the rock and slid back into the icy water. "Ahh," he said, and smiled at me as he half floated, half swam down the river. His buddies cheered him on as the young man caught up to them. The men on the raft laughed and shouted as the swimmer got closer. Finally, they were able to reach out and lift their friend back onto their vessel. Still smiling, I said to myself, "What an adventure!"

As the laughing men disappeared down the river, I had a flash of insight. Once you enter the river of love that flows from God toward you, stay in it. The river was placed there especially for you. If you become upset or resentful, you will find yourself left high and dry on a rock with your hands and knees scraped and bruised. You will see others splashing in their rivers and feel envious of them. "Why am I not experiencing God's love like they are?" Don't just stand there and wonder. Jump back into your river. Recognize what forced you out in the first place and make the choice to return.

God designs a special river of love for each person. The river of love God designed for me is very exciting and unpredictable. I have no idea how God will exhibit His love toward others because I'm not in their shoes. I do know He won't demonstrate His love for reticent people with the unpredictability of a volcano because it would terrify them. As for me, unpredictability is a thrill.

I experienced a thrill in a lightning-bolt expression of God's love in Kansas City several years ago. It wasn't a literal bolt of lightning, but it rocked my world. I had heard about the International House of Prayer for some time, and I desired to experience their worship and maybe receive a word from God. I was finally able to attend and found it to be a refreshing time with God. During a time of ministry, a prophet approached me and said three little words to me. "God likes you." Boom! Lightning struck and shook the ground, or so it seemed. Most people would have been sorely disappointed in such a short prophecy, but I was absolutely over the moon, nearly out-of-my-shoes elated. You see, during the previous six months I had repeatedly told myself, "God loves everybody, but He only hangs out with people He really likes." I believed God wasn't hanging out with me because He didn't want to, which meant He didn't like me. I drove hundreds of miles to Kansas City where a man told me, "God likes you." How could this man have known what to say to me? The short answer is that he didn't, but God did. The words were tailor-made just for me.

God has a river of love for you, a river for your neighbor, another river for your best friend, and on it goes. Enjoy your river; splash around in it. Perhaps your river has a twig over there, and someone else has a big rock on his side. Maybe yours has an eddy around the bend, and the lady down the street has a big waterfall in her river. Whatever the appearance, don't be concerned about anyone's river but your own, lest you decide yours is inferior. "Why don't I hear from God in the same way my friend does?" (Translation: "I want her rock.") "I wish God would speak to me like he does to my pastor." (Translation: "I want his booming thunder.") By now you recognize the comparison game and understand the danger it holds. It will pull you into the older son's pattern of thinking. "You never gave *me* a party." God is not playing favorites when He demonstrates His love in different ways to different individuals. To declare that God loves someone else more than He loves you is like saying a mother loves her husband more than she loves her child, or her child more than her husband. She loves them both, but she shows her love for each one in different ways. God loves you just as much as He loves your pastor and your friend. He simply expresses His love toward each of you in different ways.

Comparison games always end one of two ways. Either you determine that your relationship with God is defective and condemn yourself, or the other person's is defective and you condemn him. Whichever way you lean, your relationship with God will suffer as it becomes less and less intimate. When thoughts of negative self-worth enter your mind, or when you begin the comparison game, take steps to reverse those thoughts. Tell yourself, "God loves me just as much as He loved King David." "God loves me as much as He loves my pastor." Or fill in someone else's name and determine to move on. God pleads with you to come back into His house. Give up the lie and step inside. Find healing from the pain of past hurts. Discover a freedom that will render comparisons insignificant and allow you to enjoy the river of love that Father God created just for you.

We often have to experience pain before we recognize a problem exists. Place yourself in an imaginary family where everyone wears their shoes backwards. (A likely impossible situation, but give your imagination free rein for a moment.) Since you grew up with this practice, you consider it normal. There comes a day, however, when you begin to experience severe pain in your feet. You go to the local doctor and raise your feet for his examination. "They hurt like crazy," you say. The doctor looks down at your feet, then raises his eyes to yours and says, "I know exactly what is causing your pain." Relieved he already has an answer to your problem, you urge him to continue. The doctor simply says, "Your shoes are on backwards." "Really?" you exclaim. "But I've always worn my shoes this way." The doctor finally convinces you to take your shoes off, turn them around, and put them back on. Rising from your chair you awkwardly take a few steps around the room. Much to your surprise, you feel immediate relief, wonderful, blessed relief. Sighing deeply, you turn to the doctor. "Oh, thank you. Now I can walk without pain." You almost dance out the door.

You experienced pain, recognized there was a problem, and sought help from a doctor. Likewise, when you experience the pain of harboring ill feelings toward someone, recognize the problem and go to the Great Physician, your Father God. Ask Him to help you remove the negative attitudes that have taken over your life. The process may not be as easy as turning your shoes around, but healing is available. Cooperate with the Holy Spirit as God works in you. Who knows, you might find yourself dancing in God's house with joyful abandon.

Yeshua didn't intend for only one message to be embedded in The Parable of the Lost Son. So far, we have uncovered multiple lessons, but there are more to come. Let us turn again to the older brother and examine a new dimension to his words and actions.

Consider the older son as a representation of Yeshua. Yes, there are stark differences between Yeshua and the big brother. The older son had a heart problem and felt resentful of the favor his brother had with their father. Yeshua did not suffer such a malady, but He did reveal what the older son could have experienced with his father. The father in our parable told his older son, "My son, you are with me always, and all I have is yours." Yeshua was presenting a picture of His Father. It is also a perfect illustration of the relationship between Yeshua and His Father (John 17:10). Despite the pain and suffering Yeshua knew He would endure to carry out His Father's plan, He didn't bear a grudge, He didn't complain, and He didn't ask His Father why He was suffering. Rather, He understood the intimate relationship they shared. They were in perfect unity. His life was a demonstration of how to live without jealousy, comparison, and criticism. Yeshua and His Father were so close that Yeshua did nothing without first seeing what His Father was doing (John 5:19). "I and the Father are one," Yeshua said in John 10:30. The older son in the parable could have been one with his father, but he missed the opportunity. He was unwilling to set aside his feelings of anger and resentment.

The intimate relationship Yeshua had with His Father is available to each one of us today. Yeshua told His disciples in John 14:20–21, "I am in my Father, and you are in me, and I am in you. Whoever has my commands and keeps them is the one who loves me. The one who loves me will be loved by my Father and I too will love them and show myself to them." Yeshua demonstrated His Father's unconditional love for all His children. He prepared the way for each of us to have the same relationship He shared with His Father. Because the Spirit of God dwells in us, we are in the Father and the Father is in us. We dwell in Unconditional Love Land.

Of all the children in God's family, only one is perfect, Yeshua. Without sin and on our behalf, He suffered greatly and ultimately died to free us from the bondage of sin. Had any one of us found ourselves suffering as He did, I'm certain we would have made our complaints known. "Why not crucify the person over there? He's been rotten since the day he was born and deserves to die." From a strictly human viewpoint, Yeshua got the rawest deal of all, but He willingly moved forward with His Father's plan. He didn't grumble. He didn't become angry when He was mistreated. He didn't say to His Father, "Hey, you must not love me like you loved Noah. You gave him a big boat, but you never gave me one." He trusted His Father's love because He knew He couldn't lose it. He never left the house. He paved the way to the Father for you and for me, and now we follow His example. When resentment, jealousy, or feelings of rejection arise, recognize those thoughts for what they are. Reflect on how Yeshua handled adversity, and strive be like Him.

Our parable's older son was unable to handle adversity. It's easy to identify with him, but be aware that an alternative was available. Imagine big brother Yeshua as He returns from a day in the field. As He approaches the house, He hears what sounds like a big party. Curious, He approaches a bystander and asks what is happening. When He hears His wayward younger brother has returned and His dad is throwing a party for him, His eyes light up and tears stream down His face. His brother is home, and He knows His Father will be overjoyed. Entering the house, Yeshua sees tears on His Father's face. Filled with happiness, compassion, and forgiveness, the Father reaches for the younger son and wraps His arms around him. Yeshua's heart is also filled with love because His heart is united with His Father's heart. Yeshua approaches His younger brother, hugs him, and joins hands with him and their Father. Their family has been reunited, and the story has a happy ending.

Even though this alternative did not occur, I believe we can benefit from this example. When someone is blessed and we believe the blessing should have been ours, remember how Yeshua conducted Himself in this scenario. "My Father God is happy in this situation, and I choose to join Him and be happy as well." Don't drive the other person away with bitterness. Instead, become one with the Father. Experience His joy by seeing with His eyes and feeling with His heart.

Chapter 2: The Prodigal Son

The Parable of the Lost Son illustrates Father God's deep desire to bring His children into His house and share His love with them. God is not concerned if the returning child is the younger son or the older. The situation that drove His child away doesn't matter. His desire is that His children return home where He can lavish His love on them, where they can find peace and fulfillment with Him.

In the same way, parents are happiest when their children are home where they belong. As children become young adults and yearn for their independence, they sometimes decide to leave home prematurely. That leaves the parents with a difficult choice. Aware of the dangers an ill-prepared child can encounter in the world, parents must decide whether to turn their child loose or take drastic measures to keep him at home.

Our Father God has the same concern for His children. He knows how sin can hurt us. He knows the consequences we will suffer by drifting away from His presence. He understands the anguish a hardened heart will bring about. With a single word He could protect His children from all heartache, but in His great love, He has given us the freedom to choose our own path.

We may choose the road that leads us away from God's house and believe that He won't be concerned with our decision. After all, "He is the great, magnificent King of all creation, and we are tiny, unimportant people, not worthy of His notice. He's occupied with things like running the universe and won't notice if we leave His house." We need to refuse such thoughts and instead focus on truth. We have been created in God's image—not only physically, but with His heart as well. When our heart hurts, His heart hurts. When we turn from Him to go our own way, He misses us deeply. Just as the father in our parable missed his younger son, and just as he watched hopefully for his son's return, our Father God awaits our return with great anticipation.

God freely gave His love to us, and we are free to return His love or choose the world's pleasures. Whatever your choice, God's River of love always flows toward you, and patiently He will wait for you to jump in. There isn't a long waiting line for this blessing, and it costs you nothing to obtain it. It's free. Jump in. Take a chance and receive His love.

God's love is free, but there does exist a "love" that is very costly. The following illustration serves as an example. A certain man lived in a country where women were considered chattel, a piece of property. Their feelings and opinions were worthless. This man's parents entered into a marriage agreement with the parents of a woman he had never met. Arrangements were made and the wedding day arrived. When the festivities concluded, the newly married couple went to their new home. From this point forward, the husband confined his wife to the house. If she said or did anything her husband didn't like, she was severely beaten. This continued day after day, month after month, with no relief in sight. Given these circumstances, could this woman truly love her husband? Would she experience the freedom to become who she was created to be? The answer is obvious. The husband did not freely exhibit true love toward his wife, and his wife lived in constant fear of her husband.

Our Father God does not control us as the unkind husband controlled his wife. A force of compassion operates out of His heart, not authoritarian control, and it is always available to us. When we feel we have disappointed Him, He still loves us. When we walk away from Him, His love remains steadfast. Every time we turn to the Father and draw close to Him, He runs to us and enfolds us in his arms. He showers us with love and compassion. He puts a robe on us, places shoes on our feet, slides a ring on our finger, and calls for a celebration.

Some parents find it difficult to show compassion. Perhaps they didn't experience it as children. They find the concept impossible to comprehend as adults, let alone demonstrate. But

Chapter 2: The Prodigal Son

our Father God doesn't have this problem. He always extends compassion toward His children, and He always gives it freely. Don't fall for the lie that dictates you must behave a certain way to receive God's compassion. Remember, the younger son was rotten to the core. He despised his father and wished him dead. Before leaving home, he spoke deeply hurtful words to his father, yet he was showered with compassion upon his return. If you wonder how God could possibly extend compassion toward you, understand that He does not bestow it based upon behavior. It is extended because it is a law God has already set in motion. His compassion continually flows toward His children, and it can melt the hardest heart and heal the most broken. It overcomes miserable, stubborn sinners, and it softens their hearts like butter on a hot July day.

If you are hesitant to take that leap of faith into God's beautiful river of compassion, perhaps a heart check is in order. Has your heart become hardened to the things of God? Do His truths seem difficult to accept? If you answered "yes" to either question, it will be impossible to fully experience God's love and compassion. A hardened heart is akin to rebellion. As humans, we all have a bit of rebellion in us. In recent years, I've seen it displayed more openly and more boldly. I once watched an interview with a professional ball player who was accompanied by his parents, a very pregnant young woman, and the woman's parents. During the interview the question of the soon-to-be-born baby was raised, and the player made a few comments about how excited they were. The reporter turned to the young woman and asked when the couple would be getting married. She smiled and her eyes sparkled as she said the wedding would take place a few months after the baby's birth. Everyone was thrilled. While I understand that weddings and births are celebrated events, it seemed things were a bit off kilter. No one in the group exhibited the least bit of shame or embarrassment over the baby's birth before the wedding. The situation was what it was. Everyone seemed delighted and unaffected by the fact that it was outside God's plan for the family unit. It was an arrogant display of the sin that surrounds us daily. We must carefully guard our hearts lest we fall victim to it ourselves. At the same time, remember that God's force of compassion is always ready to reach out and bring us to repentance. This compassion will bring with it a renewed awareness of sin and shame, creating for us the opportunity to say along with the younger son, "I'm going home to my daddy. I'm tired of pigs."

No matter where we find ourselves in life, we can always turn to our Father. We see this in The Parable of the Lost Son, but it isn't the only illustration where Yeshua showed how God values each of His children. A strong parallel can be found in The Parable of the Workers in the Vineyard:

> "For the kingdom of heaven is like a landowner who went out early in the morning to hire workers for his vineyard. He agreed to pay them a denarius for the day and sent them into his vineyard. About nine in the morning he went out and saw others standing in the marketplace doing nothing. He told them, 'You also go and work in my vineyard, and I will pay you whatever is right.' So they went. He went out again about noon and about three in the afternoon and did the same thing. About five in the afternoon he went out and found still others standing around. He asked them, 'Why have you been standing here all day long doing nothing?' "'Because no one has hired us,' they answered. "He said to them, 'You also go and work in my vineyard.' When evening came, the owner of the vineyard said to his foreman, 'Call the workers and pay them their wages, beginning with the last ones hired and going on to the first.' "The workers who were hired about five in the afternoon came and each received a denarius. So when those came who were hired first, they expected to receive more. But each one of them also received a denarius. When they received it, they began to grumble against the landowner. 'These who were hired last worked only one hour,' they said, 'and you have made them equal to us who have borne the burden of the work and the heat of the day.' But he

answered one of them, 'I am not being unfair to you, friend. Didn't you agree to work for a denarius? Take your pay and go. I want to give the one who was hired last the same as I gave you. Don't I have the right to do what I want with my own money? Or are you envious because I am generous?'

—Matthew 20:1–15

The owner of the vineyard was unorthodox in the way he paid his workers. Instead of paying everyone at the same time, the foreman paid the short-term workers first. As the laborers who had started working at five came forward, the rest of the workers looked at each other in puzzlement. They became even more confused when they saw each of these workers paid a full denarius. Why pay a full day's wages to someone who had worked such a short time? They reasoned that since those who had worked fewer hours were paid for a full day, the longer-term workers would be paid more.

After the five o'clock workers were paid, the foreman called the group who began working at three in the afternoon. They also received a denarius. The 12 o'clock laborers received the same. This carried on until the first workers hired received their pay. When they, too, received a denarius, they began complaining against the owner. "Not fair! Not fair! We had to work in the heat of the day." The owner answered, "Friend, I am not being unfair to you. Did you not agree to work for a denarius? Take your pay and go. If I want to give the man who was hired last the same as I gave you, don't I have the right to do what I want with my own money? Or are you jealous, envious, and ticked off because I'm generous?"

This is a curious parable. I admit I became upset when I began studying it. Why didn't the owner pay the ones who had worked all day first? They would have taken their denarius, thanked the foreman, and gone home. Everything would have been fine. No feathers would have been ruffled. Instead, the short-term workers were paid first and everyone else got upset. Why did the owner do this?

To find our answer, look at the first words of the parable. "For the kingdom of heaven is like. . ." In God's kingdom, God's heart rules. With this parable, Yeshua exposed what was not in the kingdom: anger and a sense of unfairness. The landowner wanted the all-day workers to rejoice in his generosity. When they were hired, they were very happy. "Hey! I found work," they may have told friends. "If you hurry to the vineyard, maybe you'll get hired, too. The pay is a whole denarius." "I'm in," the friends might have replied. "Can my friend also come and work?" The laborers were happy and everything was fine. But the landowner's generosity didn't stop with the first men he hired. He found others and invited them to work in his vineyard as well. He was happy to provide work for every man, and he generously paid everyone equally. Instead of being happy, however, the all-day workers became resentful, jealous, and unhappy with the landowner.

Recall the earlier scenario with Yeshua as the true older son in our first parable. He saw His Father's heart, and when the younger son returned, He joined in His Father's happiness. If the all-day workers in our current parable had joined the landowner in his happiness and generosity, we would have seen a true picture of the kingdom of heaven.

This parable is a beautiful picture of how God operates in His kingdom. Take the lesson to heart and practice setting your heart in His kingdom. Develop a heart God desires, a heart that doesn't take offense, a heart that is always happy and fulfilled. Yes, there will be times when ugly feelings bubble up. If a coworker gets a raise that you think is unjustified, you may complain, "He gets paid more than me." Be careful. Your heart has been exposed. It isn't focused on the kingdom of God.

My heart was exposed big time when I read this parable. With a jolt I suddenly realized my need to repent. I understood

Chapter 2: The Prodigal Son

that there is a higher place to live where I could rise above petty jealousy. How I longed for a ladder to climb into the very kingdom of heaven where God could open my heart and perform His healing surgery. He's the only One who can change my heart. No matter how hard I try, I will never succeed in changing it on my own. Oh Lord, take us all higher, take us deeper, take us into your home. By Your Spirit, join our hearts with yours, Father.

The parable of the workers in the vineyard contains another lesson. As you reread it, place yourself in the story as one of the all-day laborers. First thing in the morning, you notice a man hiring workers for a vineyard. You approach him, and after a short conversation, he offers you employment and you gladly accept the job. You begin working, and as the day warms up you start to sweat and develop blisters on your hands. Throughout the day, new workers join the labor force, with the last batch arriving about an hour before quitting time. Work continues until the foreman calls for everyone to stop and gather around him. As you approach the foreman, you talk to some of the other workers and discuss what you will do with the days' earnings. The foreman raises a hand and calls for silence, then asks those who worked the shortest time to come forward. As you watch them receive their pay, you are surprised to hear they are receiving the same amount you agreed to, one denarius. You find yourself very happy for them and take great joy in the reward they have received. After commending each one on a job well done, you approach the landowner. He has a twinkle in his eyes and a great big grin. It's obvious he is taking great joy in blessing these workers. Laughing, you give him a one-armed hug. "What a nice thing you just did," you say. "The next time you are hiring, remember me. I love working for someone with a heart like yours." It would have been easy for you to become resentful of the short-term workers or to have become upset with the landowner, but instead you chose to rejoice in the situation. Anger and bitterness were given no place to grow.

Let's visit this parable from an additional angle. As before, see yourself in the position of an all-day laborer. Your hands and back are sore, but you carry on with your work knowing the workday is almost complete. You suddenly notice new workers have entered the vineyard. That seems odd considering that it's late in the afternoon. Before long, the foreman calls everyone to receive their pay. As you watch the first person receive a full denarius, you realize it's your twin brother. One of the workers being blessed with a full day's pay is someone you love. You thought the short-term workers would receive no more than an eighth of a denarius, but instead they were given a full day's pay. Filled with happiness for your brother, you look at the foreman and realize what a good man he is.

Since you have worked in the vineyard as an all-day laborer, twice over, I might add, you are probably exhausted. But you're not finished yet. Dust off your knees and hands, take a deep breath, and this time step into the vineyard as a short-term worker who has been hired near the end of the day. The foreman has just called everyone to collect their pay. On one side of the foreman is the group of all-day laborers and on his other side the short-term workers. The foreman calls your name, and you break through the crowd to approach him. Expecting very little pay because of your short workday, you are astonished to receive a full denarius. "Sir," you sputter, "you've made a mistake. I just got here." You extend your hand and offer the denarius back to the foreman. "This is too much," you tell him. Unknown to you, the owner of the vineyard has been observing the interchange between you and the foreman. He approaches you, lifts his arms, and wraps you in an embrace. "My son, all I have is yours," he says. As you look over his shoulder at the workers who labored all day, some appear upset. Frowning, they grumble among themselves, glancing frequently in your direction. As you watch them, what goes through your mind? Are you angry? Are you feeling superior to them? Or are you hoping the owner will bless the rest of the workers in the same manner that you have been blessed?

Each of the preceding story lines gives us a glimpse of the kingdom of heaven. The Father takes great joy in blessing His children. As one of His own, we can and should rejoice when our brothers and sisters in Yeshua are blessed. Be joyful together with Father God and joyful with those who are being blessed. As you unite your heart with God's, you will be fulfilling His desire. Such is the kingdom of heaven.

I hope you are beginning to understand how loving and generous God is. He waits and watches for you to come home so He can bless you. He's not lounging around thinking, "Nope, I will not look out the window to see if he is returning, because he isn't perfect yet." No matter what you have done or how imperfect you are, God simply wants you home with Him.

Yeshua continued to illustrate how important we are to God with another parable:

> "What do you think? If a man owns a hundred sheep, and one of them wanders away, will he not leave the ninety-nine on the hills and go to look for the one that wandered off? And if he finds it, truly I tell you, he is happier about that one sheep than about the ninety-nine that did not wander off. In the same way your Father in heaven is not willing that any of these little ones should perish."
> —Matthew 18:12–14

Have you ever asked why one little sheep held such significance? After all, there were still 99 sheep grazing on the hillside. What was so special about one little lamb? And how did the man in the parable know a lamb was missing?

Yeshua was showing His listeners how God rejoices when even one of His lost sheep (children) returns to the fold. God's love for each of us is so great that He becomes consumed with the desire to find us and bring us back home when we wander away. Once home with the lost child, or lamb, He invites friends and neighbors to help him celebrate the return of the lost.

Luke mentions such a party in his account of the parable.

> Now the tax collectors and sinners were all gathering around to hear Jesus. But the Pharisees and the teachers of the law muttered, "This man welcomes sinners and eats with them." Then Jesus told them this parable: "Suppose one of you has a hundred sheep and loses one of them. Doesn't he leave the ninety-nine in the open country and go after the lost sheep until he finds it? And when he finds it, he joyfully puts it on his shoulders and goes home. Then he calls his friends and neighbors together and says, 'Rejoice with me; I have found my lost sheep.' I tell you that in the same way there will be more rejoicing in heaven over one sinner who repents than over ninety-nine righteous persons who do not need to repent."
> —Luke 15:1–7

In case you still need to be convinced of how vitally important you are to your Father God, here is another parable emphasizing the point.

> "Or suppose a woman has ten silver coins and loses one. Doesn't she light a lamp, sweep the house and search carefully until she finds it? And when she finds it, she calls her friends and neighbors together and says, 'Rejoice with me; I have found my lost coin.' In the same way, I tell you, there is rejoicing in the presence of the angels of God over one sinner who repents."
> —Luke 15:8–10

The woman lost one tiny, small coin. Just one. But it held such value to her that she searched very *carefully* for it. Again, what was so significant about this coin? She still had nine in her possession. The Greek text indicates the woman looked carefully. She swept every corner, every nook, under every table, behind every chest. If she'd had a basement, she would have swept there. Was there a cellar? She would have marched into it with

CHAPTER 2: THE PRODIGAL SON

her broom. How about a crawl space? Without a doubt the broom would have been flying there as well. The point is that she looked *very carefully*, sweeping here and there until at last the coin was found. Overjoyed, the woman invited her friends and neighbors to celebrate with her. "In the same way," Yeshua said, "there is rejoicing in the presence of the angels of God over one sinner who repents." Every time a sinner repents. This is amazing! Repent and great rejoicing will break out in Heaven.

I've been to many parties, and they all include a lot of laughter. Just imagine the laughter and happiness when a sinner repents. God must enjoy laughter; after all, He created us with the ability to laugh. I know that when I say God laughs, someone will strongly disagree with me. Many believers were raised in churches where a false image of a stern and unapproachable God was presented week after week. This God, they were told, would lay in wait to pounce on the least infraction. Perhaps those who taught this image were raised with the same teaching, or maybe they were ignorant of God's true character. Regardless, the teaching has been and still is widespread, and it has stolen freedom from many believers.

My twin, Mike, and I grew up in such a church. If you've been around us for any length of time you know we are far from strait-laced. Whether we were home, in church, at school, or running around the neighborhood, we always engaged in wild escapades. Some were fun, some not as fun, and while we didn't always get caught, we did get into trouble more times than either of us will ever admit.

One of our capers took place during Vacation Bible School. True to our nature, Mike and I started acting silly during class time. It didn't take much to get us laughing, and this time we started and couldn't stop. Others in our class began laughing as well, and when the teacher joined in everyone in the room felt free to do the same. As an aside, I always thought the teacher was laughing because Mike was funny-looking. But I digress.

97

Hilarity ensued, and the sound of laughter rolled down the hallway. Before long, the teacher was called to the pastor's office where she was reprimanded for letting the class get out of control. Unfortunately for Mike and me, the pastor learned how the class began laughing, and Mike and I were the next ones called into his office. That did the trick. No more laughing, at least for a while. The pastor lectured us on how we should behave and concluded by instructing us to sit quietly in class and pay attention to the teacher. Believing he had been successful in making his point, he sent us back to our classroom where we really did try to sit quietly.

As we sat in our chairs, we noticed a couple of birds building a nest outside our classroom window. We weren't the only ones watching the process. The pastor's son was observing the birds as well. I have no idea what struck us as funny, but soon all three of us began to snicker. It wasn't long before we were full-out laughing. We laughed so hard the pastor's son ended up on the floor. It was quite a sight and it caused us to laugh even more. Predictably, Mike and I were carted off to the pastor's office, but this time the pastor's son was with us. We listened as the pastor told us how disappointed he was, and he even pulled out the "I thought you boys were born again" card.

After that experience, Mike and I concluded laughter should be left at the church door. Otherwise, we were surely destined for hell. What a terrible image of God to project to the world. Unfortunately, many grew up with this teaching. You've heard stories of plantation owners who whipped their slaves and sons alike. "You can stay here because you are my son, but if you mess up one more time, you'll get what's comin' to ya'." Whip in hand, he would continue, "You'll get a whippin'." This is how God has been presented in many churches. It is a false image, but many believers are convinced there is a threatening authoritarian God poised to beat them into submission if they step out of line.

I don't believe an overly strict father experiences any joy when he punishes his children. If your perception of Father God is that of a harsh disciplinarian, make the decision to remove it from your mind. See God as your loving Father who is always ready to accept you unconditionally. Rather than tearing you down, He will constantly build you up. If you hurt, He will feel the hurt with you. When you rejoice, He will rejoice. Grasp the true image Yeshua presented of Father God in His parables, and you will find yourself running to Him.

Yeshua presented a loving, welcoming image of God, a Father to be approached without fear and who loves unconditionally. He is safe, trustworthy, and incapable of loving one person more than another. He always welcomes those who return home regardless of the wreck they have made of their lives. It's merely a matter of walking into God's welcoming arms. I hope you find yourself at home in His presence right now. If not, understand that God is waiting to welcome you home, no matter your situation. Although you may experience natural consequences in this world for your previous actions, you will find no judgment or harsh punishment from your Father God. In His presence you will experience true rest and peace as you walk with Him.

True intimacy with God is not obtained by simply flipping a switch. Rather, it comes from investing time in a relationship with your heavenly Father. Talk with Him, laugh with Him, and share your sorrows and disappointments with Him. It's the same way intimacy grows between friends and in families. We were created to desire intimacy, both with our fellow man and with God. Our heavenly Father desires the same with each of us.

Jews have long understood the importance of fellowship in developing intimacy. One way they foster it is dining together. As everyone receives nourishment, serious matters are discussed, hilarious moments shared, and encouragement given to those who need it. It's an opportunity to get to know each other on a deeper level. We saw an example of this when the prodigal son returned home and his father prepared a huge feast for many guests. It became an intimate gathering, regardless of its size and celebratory nature.

Entering an intimate relationship is difficult because it places you in a vulnerable position. Naturally, this opens the door to potentially hurtful experiences. It usually takes only one bad experience to erect a protective barrier around your heart. A determination follows that no one will get close to you again. This makes future human relationships difficult, and is equally true in a relationship with Father God. Believing God is judgmental, angry, and unforgiving makes it difficult to experience intimacy with Him. "What if I let God down and He comes after me?" It becomes easier to shut God out of everyday life to protect against future judgment. To experience true intimacy with Father God, these barriers must be removed.

Turning away from intimacy with Father God is a form of self-protection. This leads to an innate longing for God that we strive to satisfy with other activities. We are in for a bumpy road when we choose this course of action. Compare such a life to driving a car without tires on its rims. Imagine coming across such a car sitting on a rail bed, and after walking around it you check the ignition for keys. Surprisingly the keys are in the ignition, and you check to see if the car will start. The engine turns over and you whoop and holler as you settle into the driver's seat. You shift into drive and take off. You experience a very bumpy ride as the car bounces over the railroad ties. The shock absorbers on the car are nonexistent, and every time the car lurches over a tie your head hits the roof. Your entire body begins to ache, and you develop a raging headache. You may have been excited at the beginning of your joy ride, but now your thoughts are centered on getting the car off the tracks. How to accomplish that seems impossible. Meanwhile a train whistle sounds and a headlight appears in the distance. The whistle gets louder and the light on the front of the train draws closer. Unable to steer the car off the tracks, you leap out of the car. In your haste you trip over your own feet. Somehow you manage to pick yourself up and run as fast as you can away from the tracks. Suddenly you hear a hideous screech as the engineer applies the brakes and you dive behind a bush. The sound of metal being pushed down the track combined with the screeching of brakes is horrifyingly loud. What began as a fun adventure has turned into a terrifying experience.

Life can seem like a major train wreck at times. Perhaps you have experienced life's wreckage and tried to understand without success what went wrong. Or maybe a wreck looms just ahead and you have no idea how to avoid it. In either situation, the best solution is to turn away from the bumps and the oncoming "trains" and return to intimate fellowship with your Father God. Run to the safety of His arms and allow Him to cover you with His love. He will take you in without question and change your life. Ask God to help you remove old self-protective barriers so you can experience His sweet fellowship.

The enemy will try to convince you that your life is such a mess that an intimate relationship with God is impossible. Another lie will portray God as a joyless, stern taskmaster. The best way to escape these traps is to become immersed in God's Word and in His presence until His truth overrides all condemnation. God will transform your thought life until the enemy will find it extremely difficult to influence you against God.

As we continue to debunk the lie that asserts God is an authoritarian task master, let's examine this issue in another context. Ask yourself the following questions. Do you enjoy being happy? Do you like to laugh? Do you punish your child for the least infraction? And do you enjoy music? You may consider these ridiculous questions, but they will serve to make an important point. Consider these questions in the context of The Parable of the Lost Son. Yeshua presented a picture of the kingdom of heaven with the father of the two sons representing Yeshua's Father. When the younger son returned, his father did not give him a stern look and tell him to go back where he came from. Instead, he organized a large celebration to honor his son. Celebrations are cheerful affairs, and joyous laughter would have filled the house and the surrounding grounds. Guests would have greeted the prodigal with hugs and slaps on the back, and his father would have embraced him repeatedly and laughed with him over recounted exploits. Father and son would have been near each other during all the festivities.

The fourth question was about music. In addition to joyous laughter, the celebration for the returning son would have included beautiful Jewish music as well as foot-stomping dancing. I would love to be invited to such a celebration. Without a doubt I would be the wildest dancer in attendance. As I meditated on this portion of the parable, I found my foot tapping to Israeli music as it played in my mind. Somehow, this led me to think of the movie *The Sound of Music.* In one of the movie's opening scenes, stair-step children marched parade-style into a grand, palatial room. They soberly lined up and stood at strict attention while their unsmiling father inspected them. The children were well trained, but it was evident they lived in a strict, joyless, and rigidly disciplined household. The father needed help with the children and hired a nanny who, after observing the children, decided they needed entertainment and fun. Singing was included in their new activities, and the children took to it like ducks to water. Their father heard what his children were doing and came down hard on the nanny. No more singing, he declared. Not one sound of music was to be heard in the house or anywhere else.

What a contrast between the father in *The Sound of Music* and the father Yeshua portrayed in our parable. The stern Austrian father prohibited music and joy, while the father in the parable laughed and danced with his son. It is not difficult to see which father is the most desirable.

Chapter 2: The Prodigal Son

There is a remarkable representation of our Father God in The Parable of the Lost Son. Lay aside the image you may have of a stern, unsmiling, unapproachable God. Your Father delights in you and is always ready to laugh with you. When you finally see Him face to face, He will stand with arms outstretched as He smiles from ear to ear. He'll be thinking of the amazing party He has planned just for you. *This* is the Father we will see when we go home.

Since we have been created in God's image, and since we experience a wide range of emotions, it's clear our Father God also experiences emotions. I know such a statement won't preach in a fundamentalist church. Someone might slip and say "amen" out loud. But weren't we created in God's image? I daresay some of us could use a strong dose of emotion, even if it's unwelcome. It's better than being dead and having no emotion at all.

I'm sure you have noticed men and women display their emotions quite differently. I have ministered to many people over the years and have become accustomed to those differences. Men tend to rein in their emotions to appear tough, believing tears are for babies and women. On the other hand, women let you know exactly where they stand. Tears? Fine. Anger? Get it out and done. Knowing this, I prepare for just about any response when I minister to them. When I attended a conference some time ago, I prayed individually with several attendees. One woman spoke at length concerning her need for prayer. After she finished, I took a moment to listen for the Spirit's leading. As I prayed, tears rolled down her cheeks as the Spirit began to heal her. I reached for her hands and held them as she continued to cry. After a few moments she began to compose herself and apologize for crying. I told her it was perfectly acceptable to cry. The emotion she expressed was healing and good for her soul.

When you turn to your Father God, it will be an emotional experience on some level. You may feel hesitant, joyful, repentant, or in awe; whatever the emotion, whatever the situation, God will always welcome you. Only in His presence will you learn to cultivate an intimate relationship with Him and begin the transforming process God has in mind for you.

This process occurs in our earthly lives as well. God placed each of us in a particular family where our parents taught us their values. Some of us were the older sibling and others entered the family later. Regardless of our birth order, we were always being molded into a healthy, functioning member of our family as we grew into maturity.

The similarities between growing in Yeshua and growing in our earthly families are striking. As the true younger son in our parable, Yeshua demonstrated how to approach His Father. In return, He was welcomed with love. Just as our Father God welcomes us with love, our earthly fathers do the same. As the true older Son, Yeshua was one with His Father and knew that everything the Father had was His. The two were in complete unity. Yeshua did only what He saw His Father doing. In the same way, we are molded into Yeshua's image through the power of the Holy Spirit and begin to think like Him. The same thing should happen in our earthly family. Our earthly fathers shape us as we mature, and we begin to understand that everything our father has is ours. We grow to know him so well we often know his thoughts. We begin to see things as our father sees them and to act like him as we make decisions and live our everyday lives. Spiritually, we begin to act and speak like Yeshua as we become more intimate with Him. Our hearts ultimately become united with our Father God's heart, just like our hearts united with the hearts of our earthly fathers.

To have a truly satisfactory ending to our parable, the older son must become as the Father, unified with Him as he observes the world through his Father's eyes. This should be our goal as well. As we mature, God will bring those who are lost and hurting into our lives. Because we know God longs for them to approach Him, we will invite them to come home. We will be the ones who leave the party and invite those on the outside to join the celebration. As children of the Father and as His representatives, we will accept others with our Father God's unconditional love. No longer will we be the younger son or even the older son in the parable. We will have become one with our Father God and know His heart, just as Yeshua demonstrated. We will operate as our heavenly Father would, helping those who have been rejected and hurt, those who are lost and sinning, those who are bitter and resentful. You may be the only representative of Father God that these precious souls will ever encounter. Lay judgment aside and receive them unconditionally as you bring them into your Father's house. This is the only satisfactory conclusion to our parable. If we remain solely on the receiving end of God's compassion and mercy, we will have an incomplete story with a negative ending. Instead, freely give others what He has generously given us.

"Who are you, really?" I trust you can say that you are a child of the Father, growing to be more like Him every day. As you become filled with the Father's love, compassion, and grace, invite others to join you in your Father's house. Some may tell you, "Oh, no. God doesn't want me." Because you used to think the same way, you hold out your hand and reply, "I used to think God didn't want me either, but I discovered He really does. Let me show you. Come with me and see what it's like to come home. It will be okay." With hands joined, together you turn and begin the walk home.

Are you ready to return home to your Father God? He is waiting and watching for you, arms open and inviting. And look, He's smiling. Approach Him and experience His unconditional love. And let the party begin!

Chapter 3:

The Divinity of HaMashiach

Is Yeshua God?

"Is Yeshua God?" Surprisingly, this simple question is difficult for many believers to answer. Upon hearing it they look perplexed and stare vacantly into space as the question is mentally debated. Finally, the answer is delivered with great uncertainty, whether it is "yes" or "no." Alter the question and a more decisive answer usually follows. "Who is Yeshua?" The reply comes with great confidence. "He's the Son of God, of course." True. But do you realize what that means? Yeshua is the Son of God, and you are as well, if you have accepted Yeshua as your savior. But even with that understanding, you undoubtedly would never place yourself on the same level as Yeshua. What is it that sets Him apart? I'm glad you asked, because it brings us back to our original question. "Is Yeshua God?"

The issue of Yeshua's divinity may be settled in your mind. You may have clear and definitive reasons for believing He is God. On the other hand, the very thought that Yeshua is God could cause you to raise your eyebrows all the way to your hairline. Perhaps you have no idea and don't really care. Regardless, I hope you will stay with me and keep an open mind as we investigate the issue. We may uncover a few surprises along the way.

As we investigate the divinity of Yeshua, most of our research will be centered in the Tenach, more commonly known as the Old Testament. The New Testament, or Brit Hadashah, is usually more familiar to believers and is often their only source for answers to theological questions. We will examine passages from the Brit Hadashah, but our primary authority as we begin will be the Tenach. Proving or disproving Yeshua's divinity from both the Tenach and Brit Hadashah is important, but citing Tenach passages is essential when speaking with our Jewish friends.

We begin our study with an unlikely subject: stones. You are probably familiar with the story of David who used a slingshot and one small stone to kill Goliath. We could devote an entire chapter to that story alone, but for our purposes we will approach stones from an angle you may never have considered.

Several years ago, I presented a series titled "The Messiah Stone." Many stones in God's Word are connected to Yeshua, and following them through the Bible was a fascinating adventure. "Messiah Stone" is not a biblical term per se, but a phrase I coined based on the wide range of Messianic connections. The first such reference is not Messianic, but still functions as a "stepping stone" to Yeshua.

First, we look in Genesis, where Jacob spoke a blessing over his son Joseph.

> The archers have sorely grieved him, and shot at him, and hated him: But his bow abode in strength, and the arms of his hands were made strong by the hands of the mighty God of Jacob; (from thence is the shepherd, the stone of Israel:) Even by the God of thy father, who shall help thee; and by the Almighty, who shall bless thee with blessings of heaven above...
> —Genesis 49:23–25a KJV

CHAPTER 3: THE DIVINITY OF HAMASHIACH

The archers shot at him, but his bow remained steady and strong. Why? It was because he was assisted by the hands of the mighty *God of Jacob*, by the *shepherd*, by the *stone of Israel*, by the *God of thy father*, and by the *Almighty (El Shaddai)*. This is the One who supported Joseph. We are familiar with most of God's names included in this passage, but the phrase "stone of Israel" escapes the notice of many readers.

The Hebrew word for stone, *eben* (pronounced like the name Evan), consists of three Hebrew letters, *aleph*, *bet*, and *nun*. The first two letters, *aleph* and *bet*, comprise the word *ab*, father. The second and third letters, *bet* and *nun*, create the word *ben*, son. The word *eben*, therefore, is made up of the Father and the Son, presenting a beautiful illustration of the unity between the two. This stone will become a metaphor for God throughout the Bible, including the Brit Hadashah. As we proceed, we will see how it ties to Yeshua. It begins here in Genesis, accompanied by other titles of God. As we progress, the concept of the stone will be enlarged.

> So this is what the Sovereign Lord says: "See, I lay a stone in Zion, a tested stone, a precious cornerstone for a sure foundation; the one who relies on it will never be stricken with panic."
> —Isaiah 28:16

This verse expands the Shepherd of Israel Stone. The Sovereign Lord, YHVH,[2] describes this stone as a precious cornerstone, a foundation stone. Tested and found worthy, it has been laid in Zion. The most important stone in any building is the cornerstone, and this one is precious for a sure foundation. Without doubt this is a Messianic stone. As an only son is considered precious, so is this cornerstone.

> The Lord Almighty is the one you are to regard as holy, he is the one you are to fear, he is the one you are to

---

[2] YHVH, the unutterable name of God. It is composed of four Hebrew letters, yod, hey, vov, hey. It is also known as the Tetragrammaton, which means "the four letters."

> dread. He will be a holy place; for both Israel and Judah he will be a stone that causes people to stumble and a rock that makes them fall. And for the people of Jerusalem he will be a trap and a snare.
> —Isaiah 8:13–14

The Lord Almighty said in these verses that He would be a stumbling stone. The gospels reveal that during Yeshua's earthly ministry He became a stumbling stone for Israel and Judah. Israel's religious leaders struggled with Yeshua's claims and ultimately rejected Him as Messiah. Both the Lord God and Yeshua were the stumbling stone, which indicates they are the same entity.

> A stone which the builders rejected has become the chief cornerstone; this came about from the Lord; it is marvelous in our eyes.
> —Psalm 118:22–23 (NASB)

The builders are Israel's leaders. They were responsible for testing all those who claimed to be the Messiah. Should someone pass their tests, the leaders would then announce Messiah's arrival to all Israel. They tested Yeshua, the true Messiah, but ultimately stumbled over Him and rejected Him as Messiah. Israel was expecting a "King" Messiah who would deliver them from Roman rule, overthrow the Roman government, and establish His kingdom on earth. When Yeshua came as a Suffering Servant to deliver them from their sin, Israel failed to recognize Him. Yeshua, the beautiful perfect cornerstone, was rejected and tortured until He was unrecognizable (Isaiah 53). In the same manner a construction crew discards unusable items, so Israel's leadership "discarded" Yeshua. They considered Him good for nothing. As believers, we understand the rejected Messiah became the chief cornerstone of His church, and it was a beautiful sight in the eyes of YHVH.

Although the leaders of Israel denied Yeshua as Messiah, at the end of the age Israel will look upon Him whom they have pierced (Zechariah 12–13) and ultimately accept Him as their

Messiah, their salvation. He will become the Accepted Stone. This title is not found in the Bible, but it is fitting just the same. Yeshua is the Accepted Stone every time a new believer enters the family of God.

A very large stone is referenced in Daniel. It appears when Yeshua finally returns to earth, this time as King.

> "Your Majesty looked, and there before you stood a large statue—an enormous, dazzling statue, awesome in appearance. The head of the statue was made of pure gold, its chest and arms of silver, its belly and thighs of bronze, its legs of iron, its feet partly of iron and partly of baked clay. While you were watching, a rock was cut out, but not by human hands. It struck the statue on its feet of iron and clay and smashed them. Then the iron, the clay, the bronze, the silver and the gold were all broken to pieces and became like chaff on a threshing floor in the summer. The wind swept them away without leaving a trace. But the rock that struck the statue became a huge mountain and filled the whole earth. . ."
> —Daniel 2:31–35

King Nebuchadnezzar was puzzled by this dream. He asked his wise men and astrologers to gather before him and tell him what the dream meant. These men were happy to oblige the king if he would first describe the dream. The king unexpectedly turned the tables on them with a bold command. The wise men were to tell him what the dream was and interpret it for him. If they failed in their assignment, they would all be killed. Daniel was one of the wise men. When he heard the king's edict, he asked God to reveal the dream and the interpretation to him. God granted this request and Daniel requested an audience with the king. When he was brought before Nebuchadnezzar, he described the dream (verses 31–35 above) and explained what it meant.

Daniel concluded with the following:

> "In the time of those kings, the God of heaven will set up a kingdom that will never be destroyed, nor will it be left to another people. It will crush all those kingdoms and bring them to an end, but it will itself endure forever. This is the meaning of the vision of the rock cut out of a mountain, but not by human hands—a rock that broke the iron, the bronze, the clay, the silver and the gold to pieces. The great God has shown the king what will take place in the future. The dream is true and its interpretation is trustworthy."
> —Daniel 2:44–45

A large statue was destroyed by a rock (stone) not cut by human hands. Daniel's interpretation revealed that the God of heaven, symbolized by the rock, would establish an everlasting kingdom and destroy all other kingdoms. This prophetic dream will be fulfilled when Yeshua returns and establishes His kingdom on earth. The stone not cut by human hands is the God of heaven in the person of Yeshua.

The following passages don't mention a stone specifically, but as we continue the connection to the Messiah stone will become clear.

> "The days are coming," declares the Lord, when I will raise up for David a righteous Branch, a King who will reign wisely and do what is just and right in the land. In his days Judah will be saved and Israel will live in safety. This is the name by which he will be called: The Lord Our Righteous Savior.
> —Jeremiah 23:5–6

> A shoot will come up from the stump of Jesse; from his roots a Branch will bear fruit. The Spirit of the Lord on him. . .
> —Isaiah 11:1–2a

CHAPTER 3: THE DIVINITY OF HAMASHIACH

The righteous Branch and the shoot that will come up from the stump of Jesse is Yeshua. He will bear fruit and the Spirit of the Lord will rest on Him.

> "'Listen, High Priest Joshua, you and your associates seated before you, who are men symbolic of things to come: I am going to bring my servant, the Branch. See, the stone I have set in front of Joshua! There are seven eyes on that one stone, and I will engrave an inscription on it,' says the Lord Almighty, 'and I will remove the sin of this land in a single day...'"
> —Zechariah 3:8–9

"My servant, the Branch" refers to Messiah. "The stone" is also a reference to Messiah. Interestingly, YHVH said, "I will remove the sins of this land in a single day." Did YHVH die on the cross for man's sins? Yes, in the person of Yeshua HaMashiach.

Another stone is mentioned in Paul's first letter to the Corinthians.

> For I do not want you to be ignorant of the fact, brothers and sisters, that our ancestors were all under the cloud and that they all passed through the sea. They were all baptized into Moses in the cloud and in the sea. They all ate the same spiritual food and drank the same spiritual drink; for they drank from the spiritual rock that accompanied them, and that rock was Messiah.
> —I Corinthians 10:1–4

I believe the spiritual rock to which Paul referred was the stone the Israelites drank from as they wandered in the wilderness. That rock, Paul said, was Yeshua.

Peter also referred to a stone in one of his Brit Hadashah letters.

> As you come to him, the living Stone—rejected by humans but chosen by God and precious to him—you also, like living stones, are being built into a spiritual house to be a

> holy priesthood, offering spiritual sacrifices acceptable to God through Jesus Christ.
> —1 Peter 2:4–5

Eben has been expanded greatly since its first introduction in Genesis. The first stone in Genesis was Almighty God, the Stone of Israel. It has grown to become the Zion Stone, the Foundation Stone, Precious Stone, Cornerstone, Tested Stone, Stumbling Stone, Trapping Stone, Breaking Stone, Rejected Stone, and The Stone Not Cut by Human Hands, Smashing Stone, huge Mountain Stone, Eternal Stone, Kingdom Stone, Branch Stone, Spiritual Stone, and the Living Stone.[3] All are Messianic. Many of them are attributed to YHVH as well, further confirming that Yeshua and YHVH are one.

In addition to sharing characteristics of the Messianic Stones, Yeshua and YHVH share the title "Ancient of Days." This name appears in a dream recorded in the book of Daniel where four great beasts rise from the sea.

> As I looked, thrones were set in place, and the Ancient of Days took his seat. His clothing was as white as snow; the hair of his head was white like wool. His throne was flaming with fire, and its wheels were all ablaze. A river of fire was flowing, coming out from before him. Thousands upon thousands attended him; ten thousand times ten thousand stood before him. The court was seated, and the books were opened.
> —Daniel 7:9–10

Based on Daniel's description of the Ancient of Days, I believe he saw YHVH. You may ask how that was possible since YHVH said no one could see His face and live. Exodus 33:12–23 records a conversation between Moses and YHVH. Moses asked to see YHVH's glory in verse 18. YHVH responded by passing His goodness in front of Moses and declaring His name in Moses' presence. YHVH said He would have mercy

---

[3] My book *Golden Light* contains more information on The Messiah Stone.

and compassion on whomever He chose. It wouldn't be the choice of any man, even Moses. In verse 20 YHVH stated no one can see His face and live. Moses would be allowed to see YHVH's goodness and His glory, but not His face. YHVH continued speaking to Moses and directed him to a rock. YHVH would place Moses in a cleft in the rock and cover him with His hand until He had passed by. YHVH would then remove His hand and allow Moses to see only YHVH's back.

> Then I continued to watch because of the boastful words the horn was speaking. I kept looking until the beast was slain and its body destroyed and thrown into the blazing fire. (The other beasts had been stripped of their authority, but were allowed to live for a period of time.) In my vision at night I looked, and there before me was one like a son of man, coming with the clouds of heaven. He approached the Ancient of Days and was led into his presence. He was given authority, glory and sovereign power; all nations and peoples of every language worshiped him. His dominion is an everlasting dominion that will not pass away, and his kingdom is one that will never be destroyed.
> —Daniel 7:11–14

Daniel's description of "one like a son of man" leads to the conclusion that this figure was Yeshua. The Ancient of Days gave the son of man authority, glory, and power. All nations worshiped Him, and His kingdom would never be destroyed.

The title "Ancient of Days" appears only in Daniel, and only in chapter 7. The "son of man" title appears in the Tenach only in this chapter of Daniel. Rabbis understand that the "son of man" refers to Messiah. When Yeshua spoke of Himself as the Son of Man, He was saying that He was God. This created an uproar among Israel's leaders and led them to declare that what Yeshua said was blasphemy.

Daniel did not understand his dream and became very troubled. He approached the figure of one standing nearby in the dream and asked for an explanation of the strange events. Specifically, he desired to understand the fourth beast and the little horn that arose from its head (verses 19–22).

> As I watched, this horn was waging war against the holy people and defeating them, until the Ancient of Days came and pronounced judgment in favor of the holy people of the Most High, and the time came when they possessed the kingdom.
> —Daniel 7:21–22

The following verses include the explanation Daniel received.

> He will speak against the Most High and oppress his holy people and try to change the set times and the laws. The holy people will be delivered into his hands for a time, times and half a time. But the court will sit, and his power will be taken away and completely destroyed forever. Then the sovereignty, power and greatness of all the kingdoms under heaven will be handed over to the holy people of the Most High. His kingdom will be an everlasting kingdom, and all rulers will worship and obey him.
> —Daniel 7:25–27

It isn't surprising that Daniel couldn't understand his dream. He was dreaming of events that would occur thousands of years in the future. The Beast would speak against YHVH and wage war against His people, and then the Ancient of Days would come and pronounce judgment in favor of His chosen ones. We understand from biblical prophecy that Yeshua will return to earth where He will establish His eternal kingdom. He will defeat the enemy and be worshiped by all nations as the Ancient of Days. Both YHVH and Yeshua bear the same title.

The Apostle John spoke of the son of man in the Brit Hadashah, again in the context of end-time events.

> I turned around to see the voice that was speaking to me. And when I turned I saw seven golden lampstands, and

> among the lampstands was someone like a son of man, dressed in a robe reaching down to his feet and with a golden sash around his chest. The hair on his head was white like wool, as white as snow, and his eyes were like blazing fire. His feet were like bronze glowing in a furnace, and his voice was like the sound of rushing waters. In his right hand he held seven stars, and coming out of his mouth was a sharp, double-edged sword. His face was like the sun shining in all its brilliance. When I saw him, I fell at his feet as though dead. Then he placed his right hand on me and said: "Do not be afraid. I am the First and the Last. I am the Living One; I was dead, and now look, I am alive for ever and ever! And I hold the keys of death and Hades."
> —Revelation 1:12–18

This passage refers to Yeshua HaMashiach. "I was dead and now look, I am alive for ever and ever!" Notice how John's description of the Ancient of Days is very similar to Daniel's description.

Ezekiel provided a vivid description of a scene God revealed to him.

> As I looked at the living creatures, I saw a wheel on the ground beside each creature with its four faces. This was the appearance and structure of the wheels: They sparkled like topaz, and all four looked alike. Each appeared to be made like a wheel intersecting a wheel. . . Spread out above the heads of the living creatures was what looked something like a vault, sparkling like crystal, and awesome. . . Then there came a voice from above the vault over their heads as they stood with lowered wings. Above the vault over their heads was what looked like a throne of lapis lazuli, and high above on the throne was a figure like that of a man. I saw that from what appeared to be his waist up he looked like glowing metal, as if full of fire, and that from there down he looked like fire; and brilliant light surrounded him. Like the appearance of a rainbow in the clouds on a rainy day, so was the radiance

> around him. This was the appearance of the likeness of the glory of the Lord.
> —Ezekiel 1:15–16, 22, 25–28a

Ezekiel, Daniel, and John observed events taking place in the Throne Room of Heaven. Ezekiel and Daniel saw wheels and they saw fire. Ezekiel and John observed a rainbow. You will note other similarities in each of the above passages. My point is this: Ezekiel saw a figure like that of a man sitting on the throne. When reading the descriptions, you will see that each man saw Messiah as YHVH.

Isaiah also observed activity in the Throne Room.

> In the year that King Uzziah died, I saw the Lord, high and exalted, seated on a throne; and the train of his robe filled the temple. Above him were seraphim, each with six wings: With two wings they covered their faces, with two they covered their feet, and with two they were flying. And they were calling to one another: "Holy, holy, holy is the Lord Almighty; the whole earth is full of his glory."
> —Isaiah 6:1–3

Isaiah saw the Lord sitting on a throne. Around the throne seraphim called to each other, "Holy, holy, holy is the Lord Almighty; the whole earth is full of his glory." Note a similar scene that John recorded in the book of Revelation.

> Each of the four living creatures had six wings and was covered with eyes all around, even under its wings. Day and night they never stop saying: "Holy, holy, holy is the Lord God Almighty, who was, and is, and is to come."
> —Revelation 4:8

These passages strongly indicate unity between Yeshua and YHVH.

Chapter 3: The Divinity of HaMashiach

We have observed YHVH and Yeshua in the context of the Messiah Stone and as the Ancient of Days. We turn now to Yeshua's arrival among His people.

> Again the Lord spoke to Ahaz, "Ask the Lord your God for a sign, whether in the deepest depths or in the highest heights." But Ahaz said, "I will not ask; I will not put the Lord to the test." Then Isaiah said, "Hear now, you house of David! Is it not enough to try the patience of humans? Will you try the patience of my God also? Therefore the Lord himself will give you a sign: The virgin will conceive and give birth to a son, and will call him Immanuel. He will be eating curds and honey when he knows enough to reject the wrong and choose the right, for before the boy knows enough to reject the wrong and choose the right, the land of the two kings you dread will be laid waste.
> —Isaiah 7:10–16

Through Isaiah, the Lord gave to Ahaz a sign that consisted of two parts. The first part of the sign, given to the house of David, was that a virgin would conceive and give birth to a son. His name would be Immanuel, which translates literally to "with us God." The Lord would dwell with mankind. This promise prompted readers of the Tenach to recall Genesis 3:15: "And I will put enmity between you and the woman, and between your offspring and hers; he will crush your head, and you will strike his heel." The offspring of a human would destroy the works of the devil. Yeshua, born of a virgin, fulfilled this prophecy when He completed His work on the cross. God dwelt among man in the person of Yeshua. When God gave this sign to Ahaz, Yeshua's birth was still 500 years in the future.

The second part of the sign pertained to events taking place at the time of the prophecy. Judah was under attack by two kings from the north, and all of Judah feared an imminent invasion. The verses regarding the second part of the sign in the passage above become confusing because of the abrupt subject change after Immanuel's name is given. While it appears Immanuel is the one who will reject the wrong and choose the right, that is not the case. The beginning of Isaiah 7 clears the confusion.

> Then the Lord said to Isaiah, "Go out, you and your son Shear-Jashub, to meet Ahaz at the end of the aqueduct of the Upper Pool, on the road to the Launderer's Field.
> —Isaiah 7:3

Shear-Jashub, who was with his father, was the one who would "be eating curds and honey when he knows enough to reject the wrong and choose the right, for before the boy knows enough to reject the wrong and choose the right, the land of the two kings you dread will be laid waste." In other words, before Shear-Jashub's Bar Mitzvah, the land of the two kings would be destroyed. This event was only a few years in the future. Many biblical prophecies contain elements that pertain to the present as well as to the future. Such is the case here.

Isaiah provides more information concerning the Son of the virgin birth.

> For to us a child is born, to us a son is given, and the government will be on his shoulders. And he will be called Wonderful Counselor, Mighty God, Everlasting Father, Prince of Peace.
> —Isaiah 9:6

Before examining the wonderful names Yeshua would be granted, consider the first sentence. The first phrase spoke of the son's birth. The second phrase spoke of His death (a son is given; John 3:16). The last phrase extends into *olam*,[4] referring to the Millennium when "the government will be on His shoulders." A wealth of information is packed into that one small sentence.

The next portion of the verse revealed five titles Messiah would be given: Wonderful, Counselor, Mighty God, Everlasting

---

[4] *Olam*, Hebrew word for everlasting; eternal.

CHAPTER 3: THE DIVINITY OF HAMASHIACH

Father, and Prince of Peace. The first name, Wonderful, comes from a powerful Hebrew word, *pele* (pronounced **pell**-uh). It means over the top, without understanding. It's a don't-even-ask type of word because the meaning is beyond human comprehension. *Pele*, Wonderful. He was a wonder, full of wonder and awe.

One of my favorite Bible stories includes a beautiful *pele* situation. Judges 13 relates the story of Manoah and his barren wife. They had given up on the possibility of ever having children, but God had not given up on them. The angel of the Lord appeared to Manoah's wife and told her she would have a child. She struggled with the information until the angel of the Lord appeared again with the same message. This time both Manoah and his wife heard the promise. Manoah asked the stranger what his name was so he could be honored when his words came true. The man replied, "Why do you ask my name? It is *beyond understanding*." The couple then killed and sacrificed a young goat and offered a grain offering on a rock to the Lord. As the fire burned, the angel of the Lord ascended toward heaven in the flame that blazed up from the altar. Awestruck, Manoah exclaimed, "We have just seen God!" The woman later gave birth to a boy we remember today, Samson.

The angel of the Lord had made a pele announcement. He told Manoah and his wife that His name was *pele*, and he demonstrated *pele* as He ascended toward heaven. This encapsulates the meaning of the word, and each time it is used in Scripture it is "without understanding." No wonder Manoah and his wife said they had just seen God.

The second name is Counselor, the Hebrew word *yoats*. He is wisdom, the all-wise God. While this name is often paired with the word Wonderful, the Hebrew text indicates that Wonderful and Counselor are two separate titles, both nouns. There is a comma between the two words, further indicating they should be separate titles.[5]

The third name cited in Isaiah 9:6 is Mighty God, translated from the Hebrew *El Gabor*. It means Mighty Warrior God. (God called Gideon El Gabor in the book of Judges. He, too, had a *pele* adventure.)

The fourth name, Everlasting Father, is from the Hebrew *abi ad*. *Abi*, meaning father, and *ad*, one of the Hebrew words for eternal, or everlasting. This is amazing. If an everyday writer had arbitrarily assigned names to Messiah, I don't believe he would ever have called Him Everlasting Father. This name proves that our Scriptures are supernatural.

Prince of Peace, *sar shalom*, is the fifth title listed. What a powerful verse!

> Of the greatness of his government and peace there will be no end. He will reign on David's throne and over his kingdom, establishing and upholding it with justice and righteousness from that time on and forever. The zeal of the Lord Almighty will accomplish this.
> —Isaiah 9:7

"Of the increase of his government" is probably the most familiar translation of the beginning of this passage. Increase, or greatness, is from the Hebrew word *marbeh*. Within this Hebrew word is the letter *mem*. This letter is written with a gap on the bottom left of the letter. When it appears as the last letter of a word, however, it becomes a final *mem* with the gap closed. Interestingly, the *mem* in *marbeh* is not the last letter of the word in verse 7, yet it is closed. When reading this in Hebrew, the closed *mem* is obvious and normally would be considered an error. It has been retained with the closed letter from generation to generation, however, through thousands of years of copying and printing. Rabbis explain this anomaly by placing it in context

---

[5] C.F. Keil and F. Delitzsch, *Commentary on the Old Testament, Volume VII* (Peabody: Hendrickson, 1989) 252.

with the rest of the passage. Isaiah 9:6 tells of the birth of a child, and verse 7 speaks of the increase of His government. Rabbis then point to Isaiah 7:14. "The virgin will be with child and will give birth to a son." Because the son would be born of a virgin, the rabbis teach that the closed mem represents a closed womb and is symbolic of the virgin birth.

This miraculous birth would take place in a tiny town in Israel as foretold by Micah.

> But you, Bethlehem Ephrathah, though you are small among the clans of Judah, out of you will come for me one who will be ruler over Israel, whose origins are from of old, from ancient times."
> —Micah 5:2

Tiny Bethlehem was chosen by God to be the birthplace of the Messiah. We will look more closely at Bethlehem below. Micah also said the one who will be ruler over Israel had origins from ancient times. This sounds like the Ancient of Days title we previously discussed.

Earlier, we briefly reviewed Scripture passages regarding the Branch as it related to the Messiah Stone. Revisiting those verses, we will look at them from a slightly different angle.

> A shoot will come up from the stump of Jesse; from his roots a Branch will bear fruit. The Spirit of the Lord will rest on him—the Spirit of wisdom and of understanding, the Spirit of counsel and of might, the Spirit of the knowledge and fear of the Lord—and he will delight in the fear of the Lord.
> —Isaiah 11:1–3a

> "The days are coming," declares the Lord, "when I will raise up for David a righteous Branch, a King who will reign wisely and do what is just and right in the land. In his days Judah will be saved and Israel will live in safety.

> This is the name by which he will be called: The Lord our Righteous Savior.
> —Jeremiah 23:5–6

In both passages the word "Branch," *netzer*, is a proper name. This *netzer* was to arise from the stump of Jesse, the father of King David. The genealogy of Yeshua in the first chapter of Matthew testifies to the fact that Yeshua was indeed a descendant of David. As we have already discussed, Yeshua is the Branch. He was born in Bethlehem *(Bet Lechem)*, a town filled with danger. After His birth, an angel warned Mary and Joseph to leave Bethlehem to save the baby's life. They fled to Egypt, where they lived until an angel told them it was safe to go back to Israel. Upon their return, they settled in Nazareth, *Natsaret*, where Yeshua grew up. The name of this town is said to be derived from *netzer*, our Hebrew word for Branch. It could be said that the Branch grew up in Branch Town. Nazareth was also known as a wicked, ungodly town with a poor reputation. It was so wicked that Nathanael, upon being approached by Philip to follow Yeshua of Nazareth as a disciple, was inclined to scoff at the notion. Nathanael's response to Philip says it all. "Nazareth! Can anything good come from there?" (John 1:45–46.)

Netzer is sometimes confused with *nazir*. The latter refers to a Nazarite, one who takes a vow of separation to God. Samson was a *nazir*, as was John the Baptist. Yeshua of Nazareth was a *netzer*, a Branch (or shoot) from the stump of Jesse, from the town of *Natsaret*. Some say Yeshua was a Nazarite because He came from Nazareth. The two words do sound similar, but as you can see from the Hebrew words, a Nazarite is something else entirely.[6]

The *netzer* in Jeremiah 23:5–6 above is clearly Messiah. He will be a righteous Branch, just and lawful. By His righteousness, not our own, we enter His kingdom. Messiah is called the Lord

---

[6] See Numbers 6:1–21 for more on the Nazarite vow.

our Righteous Savior at the end of verse 6. Lord is translated from the Hebrew YHVH, which means Messiah is the Mighty God, the Everlasting Father, just as He was named in Isaiah 9:6.

Isaiah contains another reference to the shoot, or branch.

> Who has believed our message and to whom has the arm of the Lord been revealed? He grew up before him like a tender shoot, and like a root out of dry ground. He had no beauty or majesty to attract us to him, nothing in his appearance that we should desire him.
> —Isaiah 53:1–2

When reading this verse in context with the preceding chapter, it is obvious that Messiah is the subject of this passage. He would grow "up before the Lord like a tender shoot, and like a root out of dry ground." The verse also refers to "the arm of the Lord." That, too, is Yeshua HaMashiach. We understand Yeshua is at the right hand of God (Mark 16:19, Acts 7:55, Romans 8:34, Hebrews 12:2), but there is more to the picture this statement creates than two thrones sitting side by side. As far as I know, God's throne is the only throne in heaven. Where does that leave Yeshua? I believe Yeshua is the right hand of God, "the arm of the Lord." There is a saying that holds much truth. "The Father loves, and the Son does by the Holy Spirit." The Son, through the right hand, or arm, of the Lord carries out Father God's instructions by the power of God's Spirit. "To whom has the arm of the Lord been revealed?" To Israel. To you. To me.

The latter verses of Isaiah 52 and into chapter 53 describe the crucifixion and suffering Yeshua would endure. When we turn to Zechariah, we read that YHVH said He would be the one that was pierced.

> And I will pour out on the house of David and the inhabitants of Jerusalem a spirit of grace and supplication. They will look on me, the one they have pierced, and they will mourn for him as one mourns for an only child,

and grieve bitterly for him as one grieves for a firstborn son. . .

—Zechariah 12:10

Again, Scripture reveals the unity between YHVH and Yeshua.

In addition to the Messiah Stone and titles such as the Ancient of Days and the Branch, God also reveals His unity with Yeshua through another amazing device: a theophany. Abraham experienced a theophany one hot day as he sat in the shade near his tent. He looked up and saw three men standing nearby and approached them. One man must have stood out from the others because Abraham approached him and said, "If I have found favor in your eyes, my lord, do not pass your servant by." During their conversation, the man Abraham had earlier addressed said he would return about the same time next year. By that time, Abraham's wife Sarah would have a son. Sarah, out of sight in their tent, overheard the conversation and laughed to herself. She and her husband were well past child-bearing age. The man who had predicted what Sarah believed was an outlandish possibility turned back to Abraham and asked him why his wife had laughed. This apparently brought Sarah out of the tent to confront the man and deny that she had laughed. "Indeed," the man told her, "you did laugh."

Who was this man that Abraham had addressed as "my lord" and who spoke of Sarah and Abraham having a son? The answer is found in Genesis 21:1. "Now the Lord was gracious to Sarah as he had said, and the Lord did for Sarah what he had promised."

As the visiting men left, Abraham walked with them. Genesis 18:16–33 records the conversation the Lord (YHVH) had with Abraham about the coming destruction of Sodom. The Lord did not want to hide from Abraham what He was about to do because Abraham was going to become a great nation. As YHVH laid out His plan, Abraham began to negotiate with Him. If YHVH found a certain number of righteous in Sodom, Abraham asked

CHAPTER 3: THE DIVINITY OF HAMASHIACH

if the city would be spared from destruction. When the Lord was finished speaking with Abraham, He went on His way and Abraham returned to his tent. (See Genesis 18–19.)

YHVH had appeared physically before Abraham. We learned earlier that man cannot see God's face and live to tell the story. It was through Yeshua that YHVH presented Himself, a demonstration of the unity between YHVH and Yeshua.

Another well-known theophany occurred when Hananiah, Mishael, and Azariah, better known as Shadrach, Meshach, and Abednego, refused to bow down and worship King Nebuchadnezzar's image. These young men were bound and taken to a fiery furnace that had been prepared for their execution. The heat from the blaze was so intense that the soldiers perished as they threw Hananiah, Mishael, and Azariah through the door of the furnace. Observers watched as each soldier fell victim to the heat and perished. To their astonishment, however, the three young men walked around in the fire, hands unbound and clothes intact. Furthermore, a fourth man appeared with them. He, too, was unharmed. King Nebuchadnezzar was present, and surely his mouth hung open in astonishment. He turned to his counsellors and said, ". . .the form of the fourth is like the Son of God." (Daniel 3:25, KJV.) YHVH, as Yeshua, had revealed Himself to Nebuchadnezzar, Hananiah, Mishael, Azariah, and everyone else who witnessed the event. (See Daniel 3.)

So far, we have conducted our investigation into the divinity of Yeshua largely in the Tenach. We turn now to the Brit Hadashah where Yeshua spoke of the Ruach Ha Kodesh, the Holy Spirit.

> And I will ask the Father, and he will give you another advocate to help you and be with you forever—the Spirit of truth. The world cannot accept him, because it neither sees him nor knows him. But you know him, for he lives with you and will be in you. I will not leave you as orphans; I will come to you.
> —John 14:16–18

> But the Advocate, the Holy Spirit, whom the Father will send in my name, will teach you all things and will remind you of everything I have said to you.
> —John 14:26

The Advocate, the Spirit of truth, is the Holy Spirit. As Yeshua spoke of the Spirit, He said in verse 18, "I will come to you." He promised He would return to His followers as the Spirit because He did not want to leave them as orphans. But first He would have to leave this world.

> But very truly I tell you, it is for your good that I am going away. Unless I go away, the Advocate will not come to you; but if I go, I will send him to you.
> —John 16:7

> I came from the Father and entered the world; now I am leaving the world and going back to the Father.
> —John 16:28

These verses are beyond comprehension. Since childhood we have been taught to put forth our best effort to understand how things work. Analyze available information and reach a logical and plausible explanation, we are told. This is a simple process, except when it isn't. It's difficult to analyze the Father, Son, and Spirit with the goal of understanding they are one entity. Because the concept doesn't fit into our logical thinking pattern, we may conclude that such an exercise is impossible.

But God deals in the impossible, and His ways are not ours. Try to explain the trinity and you begin to understand why the church has struggled with this concept for years. Many hymns and worship songs praise "God in three persons" or reference the trinity in some other way, but singing or speaking about "God in three persons" is not a true representation of YHVH. This fact is especially true when speaking to those of the Jewish faith. The Jew's central affirmation of faith is the Shema. "Shema yisrael, adonai eloheinu, adonai echad." "Hear, O Israel, the Lord is our God, the Lord is One." (Deuteronomy 6:4.) The last

CHAPTER 3: THE DIVINITY OF HAMASHIACH

four words of the Shema, "the Lord is One," leave no room for a God in three persons. In addition, the Torah strictly forbids the worship of more than one God. When Christians speak of three persons in the Godhead, every Jew within hearing distance will immediately disregard what is being said. It appears to them that Christians worship three gods, and that forces them to discredit Christians for speaking heresy.

The crux of this matter is whether God is three persons or one. After much reading, study, and meditation, I have come to think of God as one entity who reveals Himself in different contexts. He reveals Himself to us as a Father, He reveals Himself as a Son, and He reveals Himself as the Spirit. While this is a variety of manifestations, it shouldn't be difficult to grasp. He sincerely wants us to understand each one. He could have revealed Himself in ten different ways or twenty, but He chose to make Himself known in three different contexts. As to why He chose these three, I believe it can be explained this way. God established family units through which we understand how a father loves and cares for his family. When God reveals Himself as a Father, we understand the picture. Yeshua revealed through His life on earth how a son was to relate to Father God. When the Father asked something of Yeshua, Yeshua freely obeyed. The Son submitted to the authority of His Father and presented for us a perfect example of servanthood. God the Father dwelled with us as a Son, made possible by the Holy Spirit, another manifestation of God. We enter an intimate relationship with God the Father through the Son Yeshua by the power of the Holy Spirit. God and Yeshua are one, Yeshua and the Spirit are one, and God and the Spirit are one. Truly, the Lord is one. He is not three persons, but one person with different manifestations.

This being the case, why did Yeshua pray to the Father? Yeshua surely would have known exactly what God wanted, so why discuss it with Father God? Yeshua did everything with purpose, and I believe He talked to His Father to demonstrate how to approach God. Yeshua wanted us to know how to relate to His Father. He demonstrated what servanthood looks like. As we develop an intimate relationship with God, we will become more aware of His desires. We follow Yeshua's example in seeking the Father's will. We humble ourselves before the Father and serve Him in obedience. As prayer played a large part in Yeshua's life, so it should in ours.

As we close, we return to the Throne Room of Heaven. In addition to the visions of Isaiah, Daniel, and Ezekiel, the apostle John had a spectacular vision of this own that included a scene in the Throne Room.

After this I looked, and there before me was a door standing open in heaven. And the voice I had first heard speaking to me like a trumpet said, "Come up here, and I will show you what must take place after this." At once I was in the Spirit, and there before me was a throne in heaven with someone sitting on it. And the one who sat there had the appearance of jasper and ruby. A rainbow that shone like an emerald encircled the throne. Surrounding the throne were twenty-four other thrones, and seated on them were twenty-four elders. They were dressed in white and had crowns of gold on their heads. From the throne came flashes of lightning, rumblings and peals of thunder. In front of the throne, seven lamps were blazing. These are the seven spirits of God. Also in front of the throne there was what looked like a sea of glass, clear as crystal.

In the center, around the throne, were four living creatures, and they were covered with eyes, in front and in back. The first living creature was like a lion, the second was like an ox, the third had a face like a man, the fourth was like a flying eagle. Each of the four living creatures had six wings and was covered with eyes all around, even under its wings. Day and night they never stop saying: "'Holy, holy, holy is the Lord God Almighty,' who was, and is, and is to come."

Whenever the living creatures give glory, honor and thanks to him who sits on the throne and who lives for ever and ever, the twenty-four elders fall down before him who sits on the throne and worship him who lives for ever and ever. They lay their crowns before the throne and say: "You are worthy, our Lord and God, to receive glory and honor and power, for you created all things, and by your will they were created and have their being."

Then I saw in the right hand of him who sat on the throne a scroll with writing on both sides and sealed with seven seals. And I saw a mighty angel proclaiming in a loud voice, "Who is worthy to break the seals and open the scroll?" But no one in heaven or on earth or under the earth could open the scroll or even look inside it. I wept and wept because no one was found who was worthy to open the scroll or look inside. Then one of the elders said to me, "Do not weep! See, the Lion of the tribe of Judah, the Root of David, has triumphed. He is able to open the scroll and its seven seals."

> Then I saw a Lamb, looking as if it had been slain, standing at the center of the throne, encircled by the four living creatures and the elders.
> —Revelation 4:1–5:6a

Amid much activity, John saw the Lord God sitting on the throne in Heaven (Revelation 4:10). He also saw standing in the center of the throne one looking like the Lamb that was slain (Revelation 5:6). This scene staggers the mind. Imagine the many colors, a main throne with other thrones, or seats, that surrounded it. Envision the 24 elders, lightning and thunder, and creatures that almost defy description. We join John as he observed the Lamb.

> He went and took the scroll from the right hand of him who sat on the throne. And when he had taken it, the four living creatures and the twenty-four elders fell down before the Lamb. Each one had a harp and they were holding golden bowls full of incense, which are the prayers of God's people. And they sang a new song, saying: "You are worthy to take the scroll and to open its seals,

because you were slain and with your blood you purchased for God persons from every tribe and language and people and nation. You have made them to be a kingdom and priests to serve our God, and they will reign on the earth."
—Revelation 5:7–10

In the fourth chapter of Revelation, the 24 elders worshiped the One sitting on the throne, YHVH, with the words, "You are worthy, our Lord and God, to receive glory and honor and power." (Revelation 4:11.) In the fifth chapter, after the Lamb who stood in the center of the throne took the scroll, He was worshiped in the same manner as YHVH. "You are worthy to take the scroll. . . because you were slain and with your blood you purchased men for God." YHVH and the Lamb are one and the same, on the same throne but with different manifestations.

At the beginning of this chapter, we began with the question, "Is Yeshua God?" I believe the answer is an unequivocal Yes. Bible passages have been provided that prove the divinity of Yeshua beyond any doubt. Many Scriptures in the Tenach and Brit Hadashah show the unsearchable magnitude of the greatness and complexity of our Lord God Almighty, YHVH. Through His prophets and many other writers, God has revealed that His Son is divine and that He is worshiped as God throughout the Bible. Let us join the heavenly throng as they worship.

You are worthy, our Lord and God, to receive glory and honor and power, for you created all things, and by your will they were created and have their being.
—Revelation 4:11

Chapter 4:

The Davidic Covenant

What does God want? What would be in included on your list in answer to this question? I have never heard a message that addresses this topic. Teachers have emphasized what we want: God's grace, His mercy, His salvation. We want to go to heaven, which is always "somewhere out there," where we will be with God throughout eternity. The Western Church has spoken on such matters at great length. It is good to know and understand these topics, but have we become so intent on our personal list that we don't consider what He desires? Yes, He wants to be with us. He desires that everyone come to Him through Yeshua. He wishes to extend His grace and mercy to every person. But does He have an overarching desire?

The Middle Eastern Church also has topics they emphasize. They focus more on what they believe Messiah wants. Jews,[7] for example, believe that Messiah longs for the day He will establish His kingdom on earth. They look forward to the day when Yeshua HaMashiach will reign over His kingdom from Jerusalem. Yeshua and his disciples spoke of this matter often,

---

[7] For this study, the Jewish perspective will be used as an example of Middle Eastern thought.

and they looked forward to the coming earthly kingdom. Could this be God's overarching desire?

To answer this question, I decided to see how Yeshua and His disciples interacted. What did the disciples want from Yeshua? Conversely, what did Yeshua want from His disciples, and how does it apply to us today? As I read and meditated on Scripture passages, I realized I was unable to find an adequate answer.

I decided to alter my usual pattern of thinking as I continued my study. Having grown up in a western nation, I thought rationally and searched for the "why" in each specific occurrence, using logic and scientific process. When I used my familiar tools of reason, however, I hit a brick wall. It was necessary to change mental gears, but I was not sure I could "turn off" my usual methods of deduction. And if I found a way to turn those methods off, what was I to "turn on?"

My next step was to look for clues in how those living in Middle Eastern nations reach their conclusions. Before long, I discovered they are not interested in finding a logical "why" to their questions. They do not think in a linear manner at all. They focus on the issue at hand from an eternal perspective, and they study patterns of behavior. If I were to be successful in understanding Scripture written by men who lived in the Middle East, it would be necessary to consider my question the same way they did. It seemed a daunting prospect. I would have to undertake copious amounts of research as I re-trained my thought processes, but I knew it would be worth every page I turned. Suddenly, I felt as though I were standing in front of a door anticipating what I would discover when it opened.

I began this new endeavor by observing how the disciples became aware of Yeshua's intimate relationship with His Father. The longer they followed Yeshua, the more interested they became in how He lived. They noted the prayer relationship He had with His Father God and how it affected His everyday life. There was something different about His prayers. The disciples had learned how to pray from their fathers. They had witnessed the prayers of the Pharisees. But Yeshua had something they did not. Desiring a prayer life more like Yeshua's, the disciples asked Him to teach them to pray (Luke 11:1–4). They did not ask Him why He prayed in a certain way. They simply wanted to pray as He prayed. Yeshua's response was enlightening. "Father, hallowed be your name, your kingdom come." Yeshua instructed His disciples to pray that His kingdom would come on earth. Obviously, this was something that Yeshua desired, and desiring to be like their teacher, the disciples would pray in the same manner.

Teachers within the western church do not emphasize the coming kingdom on earth. Because we think in a linear manner, the church tends to center its teaching on becoming a follower of Yeshua with the goal of entering heaven. They teach that when you leave your earthly body you will be united with Yeshua in Heaven and spend eternity with Him. In contrast, those in the Middle East consider the concept of "going up to heaven" foreign. Their focus is on the coming earthly Messianic Kingdom.

Another contrast between western and Middle Eastern thought is in the way we perceive worship. Believers in the west see worship as an action that takes place in a church service. Granted, these believers may have a time of worship at home or with a study group while worship music plays in the background, but it remains a participatory act. On the other hand, Jews believe that every action in their life is worship.

The Jewish perspective of worship and the coming kingdom is based on the covenants God made with Israel, covenants they clearly understand. Biblical holy days and the Feasts of the Lord also shape their perspective. The western church abandoned the Feasts of the Lord long ago, leaving the church uneducated in this matter. Western believers now operate from a completely different paradigm, highlighting the stark difference between western and Middle Eastern thought processes.

The western church has been anti-Semitic since the second century. It was obviously anti-Semitic at the time of Constantine in the fourth century. It was during Constantine's reign that it became unacceptable to teach the Lord's covenants, His holy days, and any other matter the church considered Jewish. The church began to lose the deeper meaning of Scripture and understanding of God. As we proceed, we will examine Scripture with the goal of recapturing those insights. I believe this will help us understand what God wants, and why Yeshua prayed for His Kingdom to come on earth.

As Yeshua taught His disciples to pray, His prayer revealed a desire to establish the Messianic kingdom on earth. This is reason enough to study and learn everything we can about the coming kingdom. We can disregard how the western church has ignored teaching the word of God from a Jewish perspective, and take it upon ourselves to learn all we can from other sources. There is no denying that the gospel exists because the Jewish Son of God shed His Jewish blood for us. It is only by His blood that we will enter His coming kingdom, a kingdom ruled by a Jew from Israel, the land of the Jews.

The foundation of the Jewish faith centers on God's covenants with Israel and on the Feasts of the Lord. The Word of God in its entirety stands upon this foundation.

After the flood, God made covenant only with Israel, His chosen people, and never with Gentiles. Paul explained this in his letter to the Ephesians.

> Therefore, remember that formerly you who are Gentiles by birth and called "uncircumcised" by those who call themselves "the circumcision" (which is done in the body by human hands)—remember that at that time you were separate from Christ, excluded from citizenship in Israel and foreigners to the covenants of the promise, without

hope and without God in the world. But now in Christ Jesus you who once were far away have been brought near by the blood of Christ.
—Ephesians 2:11–14

The last sentence refers to the New Covenant that Yeshua established. Long before He instituted it, however, the Lord spoke of it through the prophet Jeremiah.

"The days are coming," declares the Lord, "when I will make a new covenant with the people of Israel and with the people of Judah. It will not be like the covenant I made with their ancestors when I took them by the hand to lead them out of Egypt, because they broke my covenant, though I was a husband to them," declares the Lord. "This is the covenant I will make with the people of Israel after that time," declares the Lord. "I will put my law in their minds and write it on their hearts. I will be their God, and they will be my people. No longer will they teach their neighbor, or say to one another, 'Know the Lord,' because they will all know me, from the least of them to the greatest," declares the Lord. "For I will forgive their wickedness and will remember their sins no more."
—Jeremiah 31:31–34

The Lord clearly stated that He would make the New Covenant with the people of Israel. Under the New Covenant, God would put His law in their minds and write it on their hearts. As Paul shared with the Ephesians, it would be by the blood of Christ that the Gentiles would participate in this covenant (Ephesians 2:13 above).

If some of the branches have been broken off, and you, though a wild olive shoot, have been grafted in among the others and now share in the nourishing sap from the olive root, do not consider yourself to be superior to those other branches. If you do, consider this: You do not support the root, but the root supports you.
—Romans 11:17–18

The shed blood of Yeshua made it possible for the grafting of the Gentiles into Israel and for them to share in the New Covenant. Paul warned the Gentiles not to feel superior to the Jews. Both were a part of the same tree, both nourished by its roots. YHVH had not discarded the Jews. Rather, the Jews support the entire "olive tree."

To understand the New Covenant in context, we will turn our attention to the first covenant God made with Abraham. The introduction of the Abrahamic Covenant is in Genesis 12 and is given greater scope and detail in later chapters. It was transferred with a few additions to Abraham's son Isaac, followed by Isaac's son Jacob, and later to his twelve sons. The Abrahamic Covenant was unconditional. Abraham did not have to meet any conditions to fulfill the covenant. God's Word was sufficient. He made the covenant, and He alone would keep it.

The Abrahamic Covenant consisted of three parts. The first section dealt with the land God would give to Israel—the Land Covenant. The second part included the promise of the Messiah. The third, called the New Covenant, was the blessing of salvation through Messiah. Yeshua's blood initiated the New Covenant. While it is important to understand this portion of the covenant, one should not ignore the other sections.

The first section of the Abrahamic Covenant outlined the land God would give to His people. This alone has caused most pastors to avoid speaking of it. Israel is a small piece of land, but it causes a cup of trembling to all the people around it (Zechariah 12:2). World powers are in constant disagreement about what portion of land Israel should hold. In the last days, this one place God called holy and gave to Israel will be the center of every crisis. We will not go further with this section of the Abrahamic Covenant here. Just remember that the entire covenant, including the land portion, is everlasting and unconditional.

CHAPTER 4: THE DAVIDIC COVENANT

The second part of the Abrahamic Covenant will be our focus going forward. This is the section that spoke of Messiah. As we proceed, we will learn why the coming Messianic Kingdom is important to God and to Yeshua HaMashiach. We begin in the book of Genesis.

> And I will put enmity between you and the woman, and between your offspring and hers; **he will crush your head, and you will strike his heel.**
> —Genesis 3:15 (emphasis added)

This passage speaks of a future conflict between the devil and Yeshua, and reveals the future destruction of the devil. This prophecy was advanced when Jacob spoke a blessing over his sons. Following is a portion of what he said to his son Judah.

> Judah is a lion's whelp: from the prey, my son, thou art gone up: he stooped down, he couched as a lion, and as an old lion; who shall rouse him up? The scepter shall not depart from Judah, nor a lawgiver from between his feet, until Shiloh come; and unto him *shall* the gathering of the people *be*.
> —Genesis 49:9–10 (KJV)

Shiloh is a metaphor for Messiah. Verse nine refers to Judah as a lion, and we learn in Revelation that the Lion of Judah is in the center of the throne in heaven. The name of that Lion is Yeshua HaMashiach.

> Then one of the elders said to me, "Do not weep! See, the Lion of the tribe of Judah, the Root of David, has triumphed. He is able to open the scroll and its seven seals." Then I saw a Lamb, looking as if it had been slain, standing at the center of the throne, encircled by the four living creatures and the elders.
> —Revelation 5:5–6a

The second portion of the Abrahamic Covenant expanded when God made a covenant with David. Like the Abrahamic Covenant before it, this was an unconditional eternal covenant.

David would not have to perform specific actions to fulfill it. God declared this covenant in 2 Samuel when He spoke to David through His prophet Nathan.

> "Your house and your kingdom will endure forever before me; your throne will be established forever."
> —2 Samuel 7:16

The prophet Isaiah added to the revelation of Messiah.

> A shoot will come up from the stump of Jesse; from his roots a Branch will bear fruit.
> Isaiah 11:1

The Branch in this verse is a proper name. It is Messiah, and He will be a descendant of Jesse and his son David.

> "The days are coming," declares the Lord, "when I will raise up for David a righteous Branch, a King who will reign wisely and do what is just and right in the land. In his days Judah will be saved and Israel will live in safety. This is the name by which he will be called: The Lord Our Righteous Savior.
> —Jeremiah 23:5–6

This verse is one of many verses that proves the divinity of Messiah. The Hebrew word for "The Lord" in verse six is YHVH, the name of the Eternal God.

Daniel prophesied of the Messianic Kingdom when he lived in Babylon under the rule of King Nebuchadnezzar. The king had a very troubling dream and desperately wanted to know what it meant. He demanded that his enchanters, astrologers, magicians, and sorcerers tell him what the dream meant, but first they had to tell him what his dream was. The "wise men" told the King this was impossible. The King would have to tell them what he had dreamed before they could interpret it. Impatiently, the King replied they were delaying and trying to mislead him. When no one could help him, the King became furious and ordered the execution of all the wise men of Babylon. Among those ordered killed were Daniel and his three friends, Hananiah, Mishael, and Azariah, better known as Shadrach, Meshach, and Abednego.

When the commander of the king's guard arrived to take Daniel and the others to their execution, Daniel asked why the king had issued such a decree. After hearing the guard's explanation, Daniel asked for and received permission to approach the king. There he asked for additional time to interpret the dream. King Nebuchadnezzar delayed the executions and granted Daniel's request. Daniel returned to his dwelling where he explained everything to his friends and asked them to petition God regarding the dream.

During the night God revealed to Daniel both the dream and the interpretation. Daniel returned to the king and told him what God had revealed.

> "Your Majesty looked, and there before you stood a large statue—an enormous, dazzling statue, awesome in appearance. The head of the statue was made of pure gold, its chest and arms of silver, its belly and thighs of bronze, its legs of iron, its feet partly of iron and partly of baked clay. While you were watching, a rock was cut out, but not by human hands. It struck the statue on its feet of iron and clay and smashed them. Then the iron, the clay, the bronze, the silver and the gold were all broken to pieces and became like chaff on a threshing floor in the summer. The wind swept them away without leaving a trace. But the rock that struck the statue became a huge mountain and filled the whole earth."
> —Daniel 2:31–35

About halfway through the dream, a rock, not cut out by human hands, struck the statue and smashed its feet, causing the rest of the statue to break apart. The smashing rock then became a huge mountain and filled the whole earth. God had revealed the meaning of this strange event to Daniel, and he explained it to the king.

> "In the time of those kings, the God of heaven will set up a kingdom that will never be destroyed, nor will it be left to another people. It will crush all those kingdoms and bring them to an end, but it will itself endure forever. This is the meaning of the vision of the rock cut out of a mountain, but not by human hands—a rock that God broke the iron, the bronze, the clay, the silver and the gold to pieces. The great God has shown the king what will take place in the future. The dream is true and its interpretation is trustworthy."
> —Daniel 2:44–45

The "rock" that struck the statue represented Messiah. Upon the destruction of the final earthly kingdom, the eternal Messianic Kingdom will fill the whole earth. This is the promise of the Davidic Covenant.

We understand that Yeshua will establish an eternal Messianic Kingdom, but where?

> "In my vision at night I looked, and there before me was one like a son of man, coming with the clouds of heaven. He approached the Ancient of Days and was led into his presence. He was given authority, glory and sovereign power; all nations and peoples of every language worshiped him. His dominion is an everlasting dominion that will not pass away, and his kingdom is one that will never be destroyed."
> —Daniel 7:13–14

Daniel saw Messiah coming with the clouds of heaven. From his position on earth, Daniel witnessed the Messiah as He arrived. Here, on this planet, is where Messiah will establish His eternal kingdom. Scripture does not indicate that the Messianic Kingdom will be "up in heaven." Rather, He will come to earth where He will rule and reign forever. This is the promise that God's people have looked forward to for thousands of years. When Messiah came 2,000 years ago, the Jews believed that the Messianic Kingdom was at hand. They did not understand that before Messiah could reign as King, He would first come as a suffering servant to shed His blood for all mankind. The Messianic Kingdom was still in the distant future. Today, Jews and Christians anticipate that glorious day, and Messiah looks forward to it with even more anticipation.

God's heart concerning the Davidic Covenant is revealed through the words of the prophet Isaiah.

> For to us a child is born, to us a son is given, and the government will be on his shoulders. And he will be called Wonderful Counselor, Mighty God, Everlasting Father, Prince of Peace. Of the greatness of his government and peace there will be no end. He will reign on David's throne and over his kingdom, establishing and upholding it with justice and righteousness from that time on and forever. The zeal of the Lord Almighty will accomplish this.
> —Isaiah 9:6–7

Isaiah prophesied the birth, death, and second coming of Messiah in this short passage. His birth: "to us a child is born." His death and resurrection: "to us a son is given." God so loved the world that He gave His Son (John 3:16). His second coming: "the government will be on his shoulders." "He will reign on David's throne and over his kingdom" fulfills the promise of the Davidic Covenant.

Isaiah's prophecy included names for the ruling Messiah. First, "Wonderful," *pele* in the Hebrew text. *Pele* (pronounced **pell**-uh) means wonder or the awe of God. He does *pele* things. "Counselor" is *ya`ats*, He is wisdom, the all-wise God. Next was "Mighty God," *el gibbor*, mighty warrior. "Everlasting Father," *ad ab*, a text that proves the divinity of Messiah. He is the eternal Everlasting Father. And finally, "Prince of Peace," *sar shalom*.

Isaiah continued, "Of the increase of his government there will be no end," which spoke of the coming Messianic Kingdom. "He will reign on David's throne and over his kingdom." When God established the Davidic Covenant, He foretold that David's throne will be established forever, and Isaiah spoke of its fulfillment. The kingdom will be established "with justice and righteousness from that time on and forever." As Daniel declared, Messiah will return as the stone not cut by human hands, and His Kingdom will endure forever.

The last verse in the above passage from Isaiah states that the "zeal of the Lord Almighty will accomplish this." The Hebrew word for zeal is *qin'ah*, intense fervor or passion, an emotion greater even than wrath. The zeal of the Lord Almighty will bring about the fulfillment of the Davidic Covenant. "Lord" in this verse is YHVH; "Almighty," from the Hebrew *saba*, meaning an army or a host. The Lord Almighty is the Lord of Hosts, the Lord of the Armies of Heaven. This is a perfect complement to the earlier name, "Mighty God," or Mighty Warrior. God is zealous for Messiah to return as a warrior to destroy the enemy, and to rule over His eternal kingdom.

Up to this point, we have focused on covenants, one part of the Bible's foundation. We have looked at a small portion of God's covenants, but the understanding we have gained will aid us as we study our Bible. God's holy days comprise the second part of the Bible's foundation. God directed the Israelites to observe seven festivals annually in Leviticus 23. We will look at one of them, the Feast of Tabernacles, known by Jews as Sukkot.

The Feast of Tabernacles was the seventh and last great feast. It was to take place in the seventh month over a period of seven days. Think of it as the grand finale of all the feasts, the climax of the Bible, a party on a scale that we can never imagine.

The Feast of Tabernacles represented two things. The first was the Millennial, or Davidic, Kingdom. During Yeshua's lifetime and ministry, Israel was under oppressive Roman rule. The Jews believed Yeshua would set events in motion to overturn the Roman government and establish Himself as King. This belief increased when Yeshua led Peter, James, and John up a high mountain. Moses and Elijah appeared before them and held a conversation with Yeshua. Luke included in his account of the event a description of the three men appearing in glorious splendor (Luke 9:28–36). This convinced the three disciples that the long-awaited Messianic Kingdom had arrived. Peter told Yeshua that he, James, and John, would build a sukkah booth, or a shelter, for Yeshua, Moses, and Elijah to dwell in. Peter had not understood what had taken place (verse 33).

Yeshua had not come to rule as King of the world at that time. He easily could have. When Satan tempted Yeshua in the wilderness, he offered Yeshua the opportunity to rule all the kingdoms of the world. All Yeshua had to do was bow down and worship the devil. This truly would have been a temptation for Yeshua. If He had accepted the devil's offer, He could have bypassed the agony of the cross. Thankfully, He said "no" and reminded the devil to "worship the Lord your God, and serve him only." (Matthew 4:10)

Sukkot's second representation was that of the marriage of the Lamb. "Rejoice and be glad and give him glory for the wedding of the Lamb has come." (See Revelation 19:7.) This may be the reason the Lord is so zealous. He has been engaged to His bride for 2,000 years and is still waiting for the wedding. When He finally receives His bride, a great celebration will follow.

A Jewish wedding is a beautiful event. Our church received an invitation to attend an Orthodox Jewish wedding when we were in Israel several years ago. I gladly accepted on behalf of our group, and we attended with great anticipation. When the ceremony began, I noticed activity around the *chuppah*. I worked my way through the guests to get a clearer view. When I saw the bride and groom, I became mesmerized. The bride was beautiful, reminding me of a painting I had seen earlier. It portrayed a bride in her wedding gown as she stood facing the Western Wall. In her hand was a bouquet of flowers. Prepared for her wedding, she patiently waited for her bridegroom. Profoundly impacted by the image, I studied it before I inquired about the price. Unfortunately, it was quite expensive and out of my price range. I walked away from the painting, but I carried the image in my mind for days. The bride under the *chuppah* looked exactly like the bride in the painting. Her dress was the same, the flowers, even her hair style. I pondered the similarities, and my desire to own the painting arose once again.

The wedding ceremony concluded, followed by a celebration that included lively music and dancing. Thankfully, our group was accustomed to dancing and we danced long and hard. The groom danced with such exertion that his clothes became soaked with sweat. Hopefully, he would not wear himself out before his honeymoon.

Before we left Israel, I returned to the little shop where I had seen the painting. I had become obsessed with it and hoped it was still there. I entered the shop and sighed with relief. The painting was still on display. I pulled out my wallet, purchased it, and arranged to have it shipped to our store in Colorado. We received it after we returned from our trip, and it now hangs in a place of honor.

The wedding celebration we experienced in Jerusalem foreshadows what will occur when Yeshua returns for His bride. Prepare now to participate in a Jewish wedding that will include a huge feast and joyful festivity. The Lion of the tribe of Judah is coming soon to establish His Messianic Kingdom.

Yeshua told His disciples and the crowds following Him that "you will not see me again until you say, 'Blessed is he who comes in the name of the Lord.'" Baruch Haba B'Shem Adonai (Matthew 23:39). Jews use this special greeting in two situations only. One is to announce the arrival of the King of Israel. The other is to welcome the groom. In the context of the coming of Messiah, both will be appropriate. The King Groom will hear Baruch Haba B'Shem Adonai. He looks forward to hearing the words that will usher in His kingdom.

We have seen that God is zealous to be Bridegroom and King. Are you just as zealous on His behalf? If you who are married, you undoubtedly aspire to the same goals as your spouse. How much more should we aspire to the goal of our future Bridegroom? When our focus shifts to what God desires, we will not be as concerned about what He can do for us. Instead, we will look forward to God's ultimate desire, that of Yeshua HaMashiach establishing His kingdom and ruling the nations of the world forever.

In addition to the Tenach passages we have studied regarding the Davidic Covenant, there are important references to it in the Brit Hadashah.

> But the angel said to her, "Do not be afraid, Mary; you have found favor with God. You will conceive and give birth to a son, and you are to call him Yeshua [Salvation]. He will be great and will be called the Son of the Most High. The Lord God will give him the throne of his father David, and he will reign over Jacob's descendants forever; his kingdom will never end."
> —Luke 1:30–33

Aware of the Davidic Covenant's context, the following phrase leaps off the page. "The Lord God will give him the throne of his father David. . ." This angelic announcement came in the context of the Davidic Covenant. The statement, "he will reign. . . his kingdom will never end," provides the reason this Son would be born. A similar passage is in Isaiah. "He will reign on David's throne and over his kingdom." (Isaiah 9:7) Yeshua's throne will be that of his father David. He will rule over the house of Jacob forever, and His kingdom will never end. What kingdom will never end? The Davidic Kingdom ruled from David's throne.

Two passages in Revelation are relevant to this discussion. The first is from Revelation 20 and describes in part the thousand-year kingdom.

> I saw thrones on which were seated those who had been given authority to judge. And I saw the souls of those who had been beheaded because of their testimony about Jesus and because of the word of God. They had not worshiped the beast or its image and had not received its mark on their foreheads or their hands. They came to life and reigned with Messiah a thousand years. (The rest of the dead did not come to life until the thousand years were ended.) This is the first resurrection. Blessed and holy are those who share in the first resurrection. The second death has no power over them, but they will be priests of God and of Christ and will reign with him for a thousand years.
> —Revelation 20:4–6

John saw the souls of beheaded saints, those beheaded during the tribulation because of their testimony. They came to life to reign with Yeshua during the Millennium. There is a teaching that only those beheaded will rule and reign with Yeshua. Upon close examination, however, the passage does not state specifically that only those beheaded during the tribulation will rule with Yeshua. Rather, the point is these martyrs persevered. Do not read something into a passage that is not there.

The next passage provides further enlightenment.

> Then I saw a Lamb, looking as if it had been slain, standing at the center of the throne, encircled by the four living creatures and the elders. The Lamb had seven horns and seven eyes, which are the seven spirits of God sent out into all the earth. He went and took the scroll from the right hand of him who sat on the throne. And when he had taken it, the four living creatures and the

twenty-four elders fell down before the Lamb. Each one had a harp and they were holding golden bowls full of incense, which are the prayers of God's people. And they sang a new song, saying: "You are worthy to take the scroll and to open its seals, because you were slain, and **with your blood you purchased for God persons from every tribe and language and people and nation. You have made them to be a kingdom and priests to serve our God, and they will reign on the earth."**
—Revelation 5:6–10 [emphasis added]

In this passage we find persons from every tribe, language, people, and nation purchased with the blood of the Lamb. The Lamb had made them "to be a kingdom and priests to serve our God, and they will reign on the earth." All believers will reign with Yeshua, not just those beheaded during the tribulation. Anyone purchased with the blood of the Lamb will be in the kingdom as a priest. According to those who hold only to the passage in Revelation 20, believers not beheaded in the tribulation will miss the Millennium. This is bad theology. It is necessary to read the entire book, not just Revelation 20.

The first verse of the Brit Hadashah contains an important passage regarding the Davidic Covenant.

> This is the genealogy of Jesus the Messiah the son of David...
> —Matthew 1:1

And who does Messiah say He is on the last page of the Brit Hadashah?

> "I am the Root and the Offspring of David, and the bright Morning Star."
> —Revelation 22:16b

The Davidic Covenant provides the framework for the writings of the Brit Hadashah. The Son of David will soon fulfill the Davidic Covenant. Let us all say, "Baruch Haba B'Shem Adonai, Yeshua HaMashiach." Come, Yeshua, and be our King. Amen.

We began the chapter with the question, "What does God want?" As we have surveyed God's Word from a Jewish, or Middle Eastern, perspective, I believe we have answered that question. My prayer is that we will align ourselves with God's desire, that His eternal kingdom will soon be established.

> He who testifies to these things says, "Yes, I am coming soon." Amen. Come, Lord Jesus.
> —Revelation 22:20

Chapter 5:

Beast

"The Beast Kingdom is drawing near." This warning resounds from Christian pulpits around the globe. Those who follow current events and are familiar with biblical prophecy don't dispute the prediction. They notice the signs indicating the last days are here: wars, rumors of wars, famine, deceitfulness, apostasy. They anticipate even more signs as they hold a collective breath. At the same time, big questions loom before them. When the beast appears on the scene will he be easily identified? What will be his nationality, and what will his kingdom look like?

These are controversial questions, but the same can be said about much of biblical prophecy. While one view teaches that the Beast Kingdom will be a revived Roman Empire, another side unequivocally states it will be a revived Ottoman Empire. We will search relevant Bible passages to determine the identity of the last days' Beast Kingdom. Our focus will center on the book of Daniel in the Tenach and the book of Revelation in the Brit Hadashah. Bible students often refer to the book of Revelation to decipher end-time theology and prophecy, but it is the book of Daniel that most theologians see as the true backbone of all eschatology. Those who have studied both books understand that John, the author of Revelation, was familiar with Daniel's writings.

Daniel recorded two visions that illustrate most of history. Roughly 600 years after Daniel's writings, John experienced similar visions. Since Daniel is considered the foundation of end-time prophecy, we will begin our journey in his book. The first vision is in Daniel 2, with the same theme repeated in a later vision.

The visions Daniel recorded present an overview of the powers that dominated the known world for almost two thousand years. We will discover they line up with events recorded in our history books. Of course, the greatest history book ever written is the Bible. It is one hundred percent accurate and provides a solid foundation for our research. Archeologists continue to find evidence that proves its accuracy. Many Bible prophecies have been fulfilled to the smallest detail, showing that the book is truly supernatural. Because of this accuracy, we can trust the Bible and look forward to the fulfillment of the end-time prophecies it contains.

Yeshua knew that events surrounding the last days would confuse many of his followers. For that reason, we must examine what is occurring on the world stage through a biblical lens. The absence of a biblical basis will lead to misinformation. Many falsehoods have been presented that twist the interpretation of world events.

When Yeshua's disciples asked Him what the signs of His coming and of the end of the age would be, His first words were, "Watch out that no one deceives you." (Matthew 24:4) His warning applies today, as deception is found in almost every area of life. One example is the teaching that Christians, Jews, and Muslims all worship the same God. Compare the fruit (actions) of the followers of YHVH[8] to those of Muhammad.

---

[8] The tetragrammaton, the four-letter name of God. It is made up of the Hebrew consonants *yod, hey, vov, hey,* and is known as The Name.

The contrast is stark. Another deception is clearly seen on Mount Moriah. An inscription on the Dome of the Rock states it is blasphemy to say that God can have a son. Christians believe Yeshua is the divine Son of YHVH. Muslims call their god Allah and believe Muhammad was his prophet. Allah, Muhammad, the Hadith,[9] and the Quran (especially the second half) all declare that Israel must be destroyed. Christians and Jews know that Israel has an eternal destiny. Do not be deceived. Know the Bible, the eternal Word of God. It alone is Truth. Engage your mind and be alert. False teachings are numerous, and the trap of deception is well laid.

We begin our quest for truth in the second chapter of Daniel. King Nebuchadnezzar had a dream that left him bewildered and sleepless. Desiring to learn the dream's meaning, he called his magicians and sorcerers to explain it to him. No problem, they told him, but first the king must describe the dream. In today's vernacular the king replied something like this. "Not so fast, guys. This is how it's going to be. You tell me what I dreamed and then you interpret it. If you can do this, I will bestow great honor upon you and give you many gifts and rewards. If you fail, I will have you cut into tiny little pieces and burn your houses to the ground. Now, let's get started. Who wants to go first? Describe what I dreamed and that way I'll know you can interpret it."

Imagine the terror the magicians and sorcerers experienced upon hearing the king's edict. Did they huddle together to discuss their course of action? Did they frantically try to think of something wise to say? Or did they stand in stunned silence? Whatever their initial reaction, they eventually told King Nebuchadnezzar no one on earth could do what he had ordered. They certainly had that right. The king was informed that the dream could be known only by the gods, who did not live among men. In a

---

[9] Hadith, pronounced ha-DEETH, is a collection of Muhammad's sayings and actions during his lifetime. The word means narrative, talk, or statement. It is the law of the Muslim religion and is second in authority after the Quran.

furious response, King Nebuchadnezzar decreed all magicians and sorcerers be put to death. While the king considered this group of men to be valuable advisors, if they couldn't deliver what he wanted, he would have them permanently removed.

When the magicians and sorcerers appeared before the king that fateful day, at least four of the men associated with the group were absent. Their names were Daniel, Hananiah, Mishael, and Azariah. You may be more familiar with the Babylonian names of the last three, Shadrach, Meshach, and Abednego. Upon hearing of their pending execution, Daniel asked for and was granted an audience with the king. Standing before Nebuchadnezzar, Daniel requested the executions be delayed so that he might interpret the dream. When the King acquiesced, Daniel returned to his house and asked his three friends, Hananiah, Mishael, and Azariah, to pray that YHVH would reveal the dream and the interpretation to them. God heard their prayers, and that night He gave Daniel a vision that revealed the mystery.

The next day, Daniel confidently approached King Nebuchadnezzar and told him that there is only One who reveals all mysteries. He said that God in heaven had shown the King in his dream what would happen in days to come. Following is Daniel's description of the dream and the interpretation.

> "Your Majesty looked, and there before you stood a large statue—an enormous, dazzling statue, awesome in appearance. The head of the statue was made of pure gold, its chest and arms of silver, its belly and thighs of bronze, its legs of iron, its feet partly of iron and partly of baked clay. While you were watching, a rock was cut out, but not by human hands. It struck the statue on its feet of iron and clay and smashed them. Then the iron, the clay, the bronze, the silver and the gold were all broken to pieces and became like chaff on a threshing floor in the summer. The wind swept them away without leaving a

CHAPTER 5: BEAST

trace. But the rock that struck the statue became a huge mountain and filled the whole earth.

"This was the dream, and now we will interpret it to the king. Your Majesty, you are the king of kings. The God of heaven has given you dominion and power and might and glory; in your hands he has placed all mankind and the beasts of the field and the birds in the sky. Wherever they live, he has made you ruler over them all. You are that head of gold. After you, another kingdom will arise, inferior to yours. Next, a third kingdom, one of bronze, will rule over the whole earth. Finally, there will be a fourth kingdom, strong as iron—for iron breaks and smashes everything—and as iron breaks things to pieces, so it will crush and break all the others. Just as you saw that the feet and toes were partly of baked clay and partly of iron, so this will be a divided kingdom; yet it will have some of the strength of iron in it, even as you saw iron mixed with clay. As the toes were partly iron and partly clay, so this kingdom will be partly strong and partly brittle. And just as you saw the iron mixed with baked clay, so the people will be a mixture and will not remain united, any more than iron mixes with clay.

"In the time of those kings, the God of heaven will set up a kingdom that will never be destroyed, nor will it be left to another people. It will crush all those kingdoms and bring them to an end, but it will itself endure forever. This is the meaning of the vision of the rock cut out of a mountain, but not by human hands—a rock that broke the iron, the bronze, the clay, the silver and the gold to pieces. The great God has shown the king what will take place in the future. The dream is true and its interpretation is trustworthy."

—Daniel 2:31–45

The curious statue in King Nebuchadnezzar's dream was the instrument YHVH used to provide a brief but all-encompassing overview of current and future world kingdoms. Based on Daniel's explanation and our knowledge of history, we see clearly what the statue symbolized. The head of gold represented the

Babylonian Empire, the kingdom over which King Nebuchadnezzar ruled. The chest and arms of silver represented the kingdom which would follow, that of the Medo-Persian Empire over which Cyrus the Great ruled. The belly and thighs of bronze represented the future Greek Empire under Alexander the Great. The fourth empire was represented by legs of iron, and the feet of the statue were part iron and part baked clay. The description of the legs and feet mark the only time the same metal appeared in more than one body part. The dream referred to the rock not cut with human hands, Messiah, who struck the feet and smashed them. This alluded to the future destruction of the empire they represent and would occur at Messiah's Second Coming. When the feet were destroyed, the entire statue crumbled and all the pieces were blown away with the wind. When Daniel mentioned the fourth and fifth kingdoms, those represented by the legs and feet, he kept it brief, choosing to focus on Messiah and His actions.

The same subject matter is found in the seventh chapter of Daniel. This time Daniel had a dream:

> In the first year of Belshazzar king of Babylon, Daniel had a dream, and visions passed through his mind as he was lying in bed. He wrote down the substance of his dream. Daniel said: "In my vision at night I looked, and there before me were the four winds of heaven churning up the great sea. Four great beasts, each different from the others, came up out of the sea.
> "The first was like a lion, and it had the wings of an eagle. I watched until its wings were torn off and it was lifted from the ground so that it stood on two feet like a human being, and the mind of a human was given to it. And there before me was a second beast, which looked like a bear. It was raised up on one of its sides, and it had three ribs in its mouth between its teeth. It was told, 'Get up and eat your fill of flesh!' After that, I looked, and there before me was another beast, one that looked like a leopard. And on its back it had four wings like those of a

CHAPTER 5: BEAST

bird. This beast had four heads, and it was given authority to rule. After that, in my vision at night I looked, and there before me was a fourth beast—terrifying and frightening and very powerful. It had large iron teeth; it crushed and devoured its victims and trampled underfoot whatever was left. It was different from all the former beasts, and it had ten horns.

"While I was thinking about the horns, there before me was another horn, a little one, which came up among them; and three of the first horns were uprooted before it. This horn had eyes like the eyes of a human being and a mouth that spoke boastfully. . ."

—Daniel 7:1–8

In this vision four great beasts rose out of the sea. The first was a lion that represented the current Babylonian Empire. The second beast was a bear that represented the future Medo-Persian Empire. The third beast, a leopard, represented the future Greek Empire. Leopards are known for their speed, and Alexander the Great swiftly conquered a very large area of the known world.

The fourth beast, Daniel said, was "terrifying and frightening and very powerful." This was the first time such adjectives were used to describe one of the beasts. With his large iron teeth, he crushed and devoured his victims and trampled underfoot whatever was left. Compare this description to the one of the fourth kingdom in King Nebuchadnezzar's dream.

> Finally, there will be a fourth kingdom, strong as iron— for iron breaks and smashes everything—and as iron breaks things to pieces, so it will crush and break all the others. Just as you saw that the feet and toes were partly of baked clay and partly of iron, so this will be a divided kingdom; yet it will have some of the strength of iron in it, even as you saw iron mixed with clay. As the toes were partly iron and partly clay, so this kingdom will be partly strong and partly brittle. And just as you saw the iron mixed with baked clay, so the people will be a mixture

and will not remain united, any more than iron mixes with clay.
—Daniel 2:40–43

The fourth kingdom was represented by iron in both dreams. Nebuchadnezzar's statue had ten iron (and clay) toes; the fourth beast in Daniel's dream had ten horns. As Daniel studied the horns, "...there before me was another horn, a little one, which came up among them; and three of the first horns were uprooted before it. This horn had eyes like the eyes of a human being and a mouth that spoke boastfully" (Daniel 7:8).

Immediately, the Ancient of Days appeared, followed by the appearance of "one like the son of man," a reference to Yeshua HaMashiach.

> "As I looked, thrones were set in place, and the Ancient of Days took his seat. His clothing was as white as snow; the hair of his head was white like wool. His throne was flaming with fire, and its wheels were all ablaze. A river of fire was flowing, coming out from before him. Thousands upon thousands attended him; ten thousand times ten thousand stood before him. The court was seated, and the books were opened. Then I continued to watch because of the boastful words the horn was speaking. I kept looking until the beast was slain and its body destroyed and thrown into the blazing fire. (The other beasts had been stripped of their authority, but were allowed to live for a period of time.)
>
> "In my vision at night I looked, and there before me was one like a son of man, coming with the clouds of heaven. He approached the Ancient of Days and was led into his presence. He was given authority, glory and sovereign power; all nations and peoples of every language worshipped him. His dominion is an everlasting dominion that will not pass away, and his kingdom is one that will never be destroyed.
> —Daniel 7:9–14

A kingdom of iron immediately preceded the appearance of Yeshua in both dreams. The iron kingdom would be destroyed, and then Yeshua would establish His kingdom on earth.

The first three empires have come and gone. The fourth empire is yet to come. Through the centuries scholars and lay people have questioned who or what the iron and the ten horns represent. Even Daniel wanted an explanation. After he had witnessed the son of man receiving authority, glory, and sovereign power (see the passage above), he asked "one of those standing there" what it all meant. This person explained to Daniel all he had seen and included the following explanation of the fourth beast.

> "He gave me this explanation: 'The fourth beast is a fourth kingdom that will appear on earth. It will be different from all the other kingdoms and will devour the whole earth, trampling it down and crushing it. The ten horns are ten kings who will come from this kingdom. After them another king will arise, different from the earlier ones; he will subdue three kings. He will speak against the Most High and oppress his holy people and try to change the set times and the laws. The holy people will be delivered into his hands for a time, times and half a time.
> —Daniel 7:23–25

While not providing a specific answer to the identity of the fourth beast, or fourth kingdom, more identifying information was presented. This identity will continue to develop as we proceed. Again, as soon as the beast was mentioned, Daniel pivoted to speak of God and His everlasting kingdom.

> "'But the court will sit, and his power will be taken away and completely destroyed forever. Then the sovereignty, power and greatness of all the kingdoms under heaven will be handed over to the holy people of the Most High.

His kingdom will be an everlasting kingdom, and all rulers will worship and obey him.'"
—Daniel 7:26–27

In addition to Nebuchadnezzar's and Daniel's dreams, the Beast Kingdom is mentioned in the book of Revelation by John:

One of the seven angels who had the seven bowls came and said to me, "Come, I will show you the punishment of the great prostitute, who sits by many waters. With her the kings of the earth committed adultery, and the inhabitants of the earth were intoxicated with the wine of her adulteries." Then the angel carried me away in the Spirit into a wilderness. There I saw a woman sitting on a scarlet beast that was covered with blasphemous names and had seven heads and ten horns.

The woman was dressed in purple and scarlet, and was glittering with gold, precious stones and pearls. She held a golden cup in her hand, filled with abominable things and the filth of her adulteries. The name written on her forehead was a mystery:

BABYLON THE GREAT
THE MOTHER OF PROSTITUTES
AND OF THE ABOMINATIONS OF THE EARTH.

I saw that the woman was drunk with the blood of God's holy people, the blood of those who bore testimony to Jesus. When I saw her, I was greatly astonished. Then the angel said to me: "Why are you astonished? I will explain to you the mystery of the woman and of the beast she rides, which has the seven heads and ten horns. The beast, which you saw, once was, now is not, and yet will come up out of the Abyss and go to its destruction. The inhabitants of the earth whose names have not been written in the book of life from the creation of the world will be astonished when they see the beast, because it once was, now is not, and yet will come. This calls for a mind with wisdom. The seven heads are seven hills on which the woman sits. They are also seven kings. Five have fallen, one is, the other has not yet come; but when he does

CHAPTER 5: BEAST

come, he must remain for only a little while. The beast who once was, and now is not, is an eighth king. He belongs to the seven and is going to his destruction.

"The ten horns you saw are ten kings who have not yet received a kingdom, but who for one hour will receive authority as kings along with the beast. They have one purpose and will give their power and authority to the beast. They will wage war against the Lamb, but the Lamb will triumph over them because he is Lord of lords and King of kings—and with him will be his called, chosen and faithful followers."
—Revelation 17:1–14

John saw a scarlet beast with seven heads and ten horns that was covered with blasphemous names. This was an expansion of Daniel's description of the beast. John repeated Daniel's earlier statements that the beast represented a kingdom that was, now is not, but will rise again. John described a scene with a beast. Sitting upon this beast was a prostitute, drunk on the blood of God's holy people, representing a terrible persecution of the saints before Yeshua's return.

John was more descriptive of the beast in verses 7–14 and includes the statement, "this calls for a mind with wisdom."[10] Verses 10–11 state, "Five [kings] have fallen, one is, the other has not yet come; but when he does come, he must remain for only a little while. The beast who once was, and now is not, is an eighth king. He belongs to the seven and is going to his destruction." The five fallen kingdoms once ruled over Israel. They included Egypt, Assyria, Babylon, Medo-Persia, and the Greeks. John was looking back in history. The phrase "one is" referred to the Roman Empire which dominated the world at the time John was writing. That would have been the sixth king. "The other has not yet come" would be number seven, and the eighth would come out of the seventh.

---

[10] Much of what I will present here was first explained to me by Walid Shoebat, a Palestinian American speaker and author. Once a Muslim, he is now a Christian.

At the beginning of this chapter, I stated that many Bible students believe the beast will be a revived Roman Empire. Before we accept that as true, we must look at Italy, the seat of the old Roman Empire. Several observations regarding this premise are problematic. For instance, the residents of Italy today are called Italians, not Romans. While the Romans of old frightened everyone, today's Italians aren't threatening anyone. In addition, the old Roman Empire was wealthy; today, Italy struggles to meet its financial obligations. The Roman Empire was large, while Italy is comparatively small. It doesn't appear likely that Italy will be a threat to anyone, much less rise to the status of a soon-coming world-dominating kingdom.

In addition to examining Italy, there is the issue of the ten horns who have not yet received a kingdom (verse 12). Over the last 40 to 50 years, we have been taught that these horns represent the European Union. The prevailing notion has been that ten European nations will unite against Israel. This theory can also be challenged. Consider the nations that comprise the European Union today. There is not one that resembles a conquering kingdom.

Considering these observations, do we continue to consider the revived Roman Empire theory? Or do we place the preceding Bible passages into historical context to see if there is an alternative interpretation? Since the former is doubtful, let us pursue the latter.

As John wrote the book of Revelation, the Roman Empire was still very strong. After the fall of the Roman Empire, history tells us the Turks ruled the area where Israel had been located. During the early centuries AD, the Turks became prominent and began to appropriate large portions of land. They were a brutal people who imposed their Muslim beliefs on everyone under their rule. As a result, the Catholic Church began to organize fighting forces from Europe. Several armies were sent to liberate Jerusalem from tyrannical Muslim control. These religious wars

CHAPTER 5: BEAST

became known as the Crusades. As the Turks' territory grew, their power increased. They became known formally as the Ottoman Empire about 1300AD.

We'll interrupt the history lesson to read the information John provided about the beast.

> The dragon stood on the shore of the sea. And I saw a beast coming out of the sea. It had ten horns and seven heads, with ten crowns on its horns, and on each head a blasphemous name. The beast I saw resembled a leopard, but had feet like those of a bear and a mouth like that of a lion. The dragon gave the beast his power and his throne and great authority. **One of the heads of the beast seemed to have had a fatal wound, but the fatal wound had been healed.** The whole world was filled with wonder and followed the beast. People worshiped the dragon because he had given authority to the beast, and they also worshiped the beast and asked, "Who is like the beast? Who can wage war against it?"
> —Revelation 13:1–4 (emphasis added)

In Revelation 17, we read that the seven heads represented seven kings. The passage in the 13th chapter revealed that one of the heads of the beast sustained a fatal wound. Only here in the Bible do we learn this information. It would be logical to conclude that one of the empires "died" after receiving a fatal wound. The wound healed, indicating the empire was revitalized and came back to life.

Armed with this information, we return to history. We left off with the Ottoman Empire, the roots of which stretched back hundreds of years, with its formal establishment about 1300AD. The empire covered a large area comprised of southeast Europe, northern Africa, and western Asia, and dominated the region for over 600 years. The Ottoman army joined Germany in World War I and was defeated in 1918 by allied forces. As a result, the Ottoman Empire was divided into little pieces and distributed among other countries, including Britain and France. The Balfour

Declaration granted Britain the territory we know as Israel. After roughly ten years of political maneuverings and bloody nationalist movements, the caliphate was abolished.[11]

The Ottoman Empire had sustained a fatal head wound. If we are to consider that this empire is the seventh kingdom spoken of by Daniel and John, and if the eighth is to come out of it, then it must come back to life (Revelation 17:11). Are there signs today that indicate its revival?

As a matter of fact, there are. While there may be earlier signs, the first one I recall occurred in my youth. In the mid-1960s, world-famous boxer Cassius Clay changed his name to Muhammad Ali. I didn't understand why someone would change his name, especially to one that was Muslim. I asked my mother about it, and she told me the boxer had become a Muslim and wanted his name to reflect his new religion. Muslims were influencing people even then, and through the years, their influence has spread. They have an especially strong presence in prisons where a captive audience exists. Many references are made to Islam in today's news, whether directly or indirectly. The Middle East is a hotbed of conflict due to prevalent Islamic teachings. Dozens of people are put to death daily for disobeying the tenets of Islam. It is a religion where murderous acts are considered godly and even rewarded. Lies are acceptable if they accomplish a perceived goal. When the Taliban took over Afghanistan in 2021, the country's name was changed to the Islamic Emirate of Afghanistan. It is no secret that Muslims are working to establish a working caliphate once again. These activities point to a potential rebirth of the Ottoman Empire.

In addition to the seven heads that symbolize seven kingdoms, there is the subject of the ten toes of iron that Nebuchadnezzar saw on the statue in his dream. They were part iron (perhaps representing Sunni Muslims) and part clay (perhaps representing

---

[11] An Islamic state government under a caliph (the supreme religious and political leader).

Shia Muslims). I believe the ten toes may represent ten nations that surround Israel, all Islamic and all anti-Israel.

Considering these historical points and placing them in a biblical context, it becomes difficult to align them with a revived Roman Empire. It simply doesn't fit. Inserting a revived Ottoman Empire into the picture permits the pieces of the puzzle to fall into place.

To further cement this conclusion, we find another critical piece of evidence in the book of Daniel.

> "Know and understand this: From the time the word goes out to restore and rebuild Jerusalem until the Anointed One, the ruler, comes, there will be seven 'sevens,' and sixty-two 'sevens.' It will be rebuilt with streets and a trench, but in times of trouble. After the sixty-two 'sevens,' the Anointed One will be put to death and will have nothing. The people of the ruler who will come will destroy the city and the sanctuary.
> —Daniel 9:25–26a

This passage refers to what is commonly called the 70 weeks of Daniel, a countdown to the return of Messiah and what will occur afterward. The 70 weeks are divided into three parts. The first is seven "sevens" that comprise 49 years. According to Daniel, Jerusalem would be rebuilt during these turbulent years. The countdown for this period began with the decree that authorized Nehemiah to go to Jerusalem to rebuild its walls and restore its gates. (See Nehemiah 2.)

The second portion of the 70 weeks is sixty-two "sevens." This is the 434-year period between the rebuilding of Jerusalem and Messiah's triumphal entry into Jerusalem. It was exactly 483 years, 434 plus 49, from the time of the decree to rebuild Jerusalem to the triumphal entry, just as Daniel prophesied. When Messiah rode into Jerusalem, everyone shouted, "Hosanna to the Son of David." Matthew wrote that the events of the day fulfilled Zechariah's prophecy: "Say to Daughter Zion, See your king comes to you, gentle and riding on a donkey, and on a colt, the foal of a donkey." (Matthew 21:5, Zechariah 9:9.) Messiah was hailed as King, the only occasion when He was exalted as king while on earth. A few days later Jewish leaders called for His execution. Daniel said in verse 26 of chapter 9, "After the sixty-two 'sevens,' the Anointed One will be cut off, but not for himself."

In the same verse, Daniel made a particularly revealing statement that is often misinterpreted. "The people of the ruler who will come will destroy the city and the sanctuary." The "ruler who will come" is a reference to the beast. The people who would destroy the city and the sanctuary would be the same people group out of which the future beast would arise. The prevailing teaching has been that the Romans destroyed the Temple. In one sense that is correct, but look at the broader picture. Because the vast Roman Empire required a large militia, the government conscripted soldiers from the lands they had conquered. The soldiers of the 10th Legion of the Roman Empire who marched into Jerusalem in 70AD were Syrians and Turks, not Romans. They were dispatched by Rome to destroy Jerusalem, but they were to leave the Temple intact. Emotions overcame reason, and both the city and the sanctuary were destroyed as Daniel had foreseen. Syria and Turkey later became the central part of the Ottoman Empire, an area that will once again rise to prominence in the last days. The beast will emerge out of this revived empire.

Return to Revelation 17. As we read this chapter and the next, understand that chapter 17 speaks of a spiritual Babylon while chapter 18 describes a materialistic Babylon.

> One of the seven angels who had the seven bowls came and said to me, 'Come, I will show you the punishment of the great prostitute, who sits by many waters. . . Then the angel carried me away in the Spirit into a desert. There I saw a woman sitting on a scarlet beast that was

CHAPTER 5: BEAST

covered with blasphemous names and had seven heads and ten horns.
—Revelation 17:1, 3

After this I saw another angel coming down from heaven. He had great authority, and the earth was illuminated by his splendour. With a mighty voice he shouted: '"Fallen! Fallen is Babylon the Great!"
—Revelation 18:1–2a

The last sentence is quoted from a prophecy in Isaiah.

A prophecy against the Desert by the Sea: Like whirlwinds sweeping through the southland, an invader comes from the desert, from a land of terror. A dire vision has been shown to me... Look, here comes a man in a chariot with a team of horses. And he gives back the answer: "Babylon has fallen, has fallen!"
—Isaiah 21:1–2a, 9a

The "Desert by the Sea" spoken of by Isaiah is Babylon. But, you say, Babylon is not a desert, and it is not by the sea. "Babylon" is sometimes used as a metaphor for evil in the Bible. It is also used to indicate an area we know today as Saudi Arabia, which is the case here. Most of this country is a desert, and it is located by the sea.

The "prostitute" in Revelation 17 and "Babylon the Great" in Revelation 18 refer to the same entity, Babylon. In Revelation 17, she was drunk with the blood of the saints and the abominations of the earth (verse 6). In chapter 18, she was very wealthy and held the merchants of the world in the palm of her hand (verse 9). It seemed she held all the power. John, however, went on to report the fall of Babylon and detailed the scope of her destruction. In the end she was consumed by fire.

I mentioned earlier that Revelation 17 and 18 spoke of a spiritual Babylon and a materialistic Babylon respectively. Saudi Arabia has elements of both. Spiritually, the seat of religious Islam, Mecca, is in Saudi Arabia. It is highly revered by Muslims.

Materially, Saudi Arabia is beyond rich due to oil deposits under its land. As one of the founding members of OPEC, it plays an important role in determining how much oil is produced for world-wide consumption as well as how much it will cost. Eventually, the fountain of oil will be turned off and the merchants of the world will weep. A great depression will encompass the globe. Ultimately, the land will be consumed by fire, and the smoke from its burning will go up forever as the underground supply of oil burns.

> Then the angel said to me, 'The waters you saw, where the prostitute sits, are peoples, multitudes, nations and languages. The beast and the ten horns you saw will hate the prostitute. They will bring her to ruin and leave her naked; they will eat her flesh and burn her with fire. For God has put it into their hearts to accomplish his purpose by agreeing to hand over to the beast their royal authority, until God's words are fulfilled. The woman you saw is the great city that rules over the kings of the earth.'
> —Revelation 17:15–18

The beast, a revived Ottoman Empire, will kill Babylon the Prostitute. The Turks hate Saudi Arabia. They take strong exception to the fact that Saudi Arabia conducts business with the West, especially with the Great Satan, America. Saudi Arabia has become rich while most Arabs outside the country are poor. Strong resentment will cause the beast to set himself against Saudi Arabia and cause widespread destruction. The holy site of Mecca will be ruined, leaving no sanctuary for the beast. His attention will turn to Jerusalem. There he will enter the temple and claim it as his own. "Who is like the beast? Who can wage war against it?" (Revelation 13:4.) Everything will be in place for the "abomination of desolation" spoken of by Daniel, and pagan sacrifices will be offered in the Jewish Temple (Daniel 12:11).

Islam is a brutal religion. Numerous stories circulate that detail beheadings conducted by militant Islamic groups. The executions are carried out in public, recorded, and often posted on the internet for millions to view. One militant Islamic group that controls about a third of Syria and Iraq has established a direct affiliate less than 500 miles from the southern tip of Italy. One group member let the cat out of the bag when he said they planned to conquer Rome, providing further evidence that the beast of the final days will not be a revived Roman Empire.

Beheading seems to be Islam's favored method of execution. Classes are offered in how to carry out the procedure, a clear indication of the times in which we live. This barbaric method of execution is mentioned by John in Revelation.

> I saw thrones on which were seated those who had been given authority to judge. And I saw the souls of those who had been beheaded because of their testimony about Jesus and because of the word of God.
> —Revelation 20:4a

It is critical to pray for Muslims. Ask YHVH to reveal to the followers of Islam the truth of the Gospel. Pray for their salvation. Inform others about Islam. Soon, the stone not cut by human hands will smash the beast kingdom. As believers in Yeshua, we long for all Muslims to be saved from destruction. Yes, a number have received salvation, but many more desperately need to hear the good news of Yeshua HaMashiach.

Islam is now the fastest growing religion in the world, making this another reason to pray for Muslims. Christianity still has the most adherents world-wide, but Islam outpaces Christianity in growth and is increasing at more than twice the rate of the world's population. The Pew Research Center estimates that the number of Muslims will surpass the number of Christians in the second half of 21st century.[12] This increase can be attributed to a couple of things. First, the birth rate for Muslims is much

---

[12] Stimage, Kaitlyn. "The Fastest Growing Religions in the World." WorldAtlas.com, 20 June 2019, www.WorldAtlas.com/articles/the-fastest-growing-religions-in-the-world.html.

higher than that of any other religious group. Second, the number of people converting to Islam is increasing rapidly.

So far, we have thoroughly investigated the identity of the last days' beast kingdom. When placing our Bible research in the context of history, I believe the conclusions we have reached are valid. Others who share this view include well-known names such as John Wesley, Vernon Richards, Sir Robert Anderson, Martin Luther, John Calvin, and Jonathan Edwards. They all taught that Islam would be the beast kingdom of the last days. As you proceed with your study of end-time events, consider the information we have covered in this chapter.

There is one more matter to consider before concluding, and that is the issue of "all nations." When the Bible says all nations, the whole earth, the whole world, or all people, what exactly does that mean? For example, in Revelation 13:8 John said all inhabitants of the earth whose names are not written in the Lamb's book of life would worship the beast. In verse 12, the second beast will appear and make the earth and its inhabitants worship the first beast. All the inhabitants of the earth will be deceived (verse 14). All people will be forced to receive a mark on their right hands or on their foreheads (verse 16).

We interpret these passages in the context of our culture and language, assuming "all" means everyone in existence. It is customary for us to assume that all nations, or the whole world, are being referenced. Rather than making a blind assumption, it would be beneficial to investigate what "all the earth" meant in Bible times. What did their world look like? They obviously didn't hold our world view. In many ways we live in a global society, a far cry from how the world was perceived in Bible times. Seldom does the phrase "all the world" encompass the entire planet when biblical authors used such words. Rather, this and similar phrases were used as hyperbole to make an emphatic statement.

CHAPTER 5: BEAST

As an example, read the following passage. Daniel was speaking to King Belshazzar about the king's father:

> "Your Majesty, the Most High God gave your father Nebuchadnezzar sovereignty and greatness and glory and splendor. Because of the high position he gave him, all the nations and peoples of every language dreaded and feared him.
> —Daniel 5:18–19a

"All the nations" was comprised of countries around Babylon. Those who lived in the land that would one day be known as Australia would not have feared Nebuchadnezzar.

> From all nations people came to listen to Solomon's wisdom, sent by all the kings of the world, who had heard of his wisdom.
> —1 Kings 4:34

"All nations" in this passage would have been areas where people had access to camels as a mode of transportation.

> Howbeit every nation made gods of their own, and put them in the houses of the high places which the Samaritans had made, every nation in their cities wherein they dwelt.
> —2 Kings 17:29 (KJV)

The idol-making business was taking place in northern Israel. "Every nation" placed them in the houses of the high places the Samaritans built. It's safe to say "every nation" applied to the nations in the region. Any population living in what would one day be known as Iceland wouldn't have placed idols in Israel.

> "It is true, Lord, that the Assyrian kings have laid waste all these peoples and their lands."
> —Isaiah 37:18

Who, exactly, were the kings of Assyria laying waste to? It was only to a portion of the Middle East.

> As I was thinking about this, suddenly a goat with a prominent horn between its eyes came from the west, crossing the whole earth without touching the ground.
> —Daniel 8:5

This portion of Daniel's prophecy pertains to Alexander the Great and the Greek Empire. Maps that illustrate the breadth of the Greek Empire clearly do not show a planet-wide occupation.

> A prophecy: The word of the Lord concerning Israel. The Lord, who stretches out the heavens, who lays the foundation of the earth, and who forms the human spirit within a person, declares: "I am going to make Jerusalem a cup that sends all the surrounding peoples reeling. Judah will be besieged as well as Jerusalem. On that day, when all the nations of the earth are gathered against her, I will make Jerusalem an immovable rock for all the nations.
> —Zechariah 12:1–3a

The phrase "all the surrounding peoples" in the above passage explains exactly who would be affected. "All the nations of the earth" is once again used as hyperbole.

> In those days and at that time, when I restore the fortunes of Judah and Jerusalem, I will gather all nations and bring them down to the Valley of Jehoshaphat. There I will put them on trial for what they did to my inheritance, my people Israel... Let the nations be roused; let them advance into the Valley of Jehoshaphat, for there I will sit to judge all the nations on every side.
> —Joel 3:1–2a, 12

Again, this would concern the known world at that time.

"The whole world" appears at the final battle before the return of Yeshua HaMashiach, John tells us:

> Then I saw three impure spirits that looked like frogs; they came out of the mouth of the dragon, out of the mouth of the beast and out of the mouth of the false prophet. They are demonic spirits that perform signs,

and they go out to the kings of the whole world, to gather them for the battle on the great day of God Almighty. 'Look, I come like a thief! Blessed is the one who stays awake and remains clothed, so as not to go naked and be shamefully exposed.' Then they gathered the kings together to the place that in Hebrew is called Armageddon.
—Revelation 16:13–16

If you have been to Israel, you know how small the Valley of Megiddo is. Imagine the armies of "the whole world" gathering there. Each soldier would have less than one square inch of land on which to stand. It is more likely that "the whole world" will be made up of soldiers from Syria, Turkey, and other Islamic countries.

In summary, "all the world" or "all the nations" generally refers to the surrounding area, namely the Middle East. Simply substitute "all the surrounding nations" for these phrases and a clearer understanding of the passage emerges.

These points provide hope that America is not doomed. How often have you assumed America is included in the verse that says all nations who turn against Israel will be destroyed? When substituting the phrase "all the surrounding nations," it becomes apparent we would be excluded. We are a long way from Israel. As a nation, we don't have to turn against Israel. Rather, we can bless Israel and become a sheep nation blessed by God. This may cause Muslims in our country to arise in strong disagreement to our actions, but how far would they go to stop us? They may cause enough fear to exert some control over the citizenry, but that doesn't mean they will conquer the "whole world." Be encouraged. Hold fast to hope. Regardless of what you see or hear in these last days that strikes fear in your heart, stand firm on the rock of your salvation. Amen.

Come, Yeshua HaMashiach.

Chapter 6:

Rebuild the Temple

"Rebuild the Temple? Why? The Temple isn't relevant today. I mean, that whole system of offering sacrifices is no longer necessary, right? Besides, we are the temple of the Holy Spirit. Who needs a building?" Perplexed, Bob turned to Norm who had just told him about an online news article. Plans were in place to rebuild the Temple in Jerusalem.

Norm replied, "Well, Bob, it seems the plans have been drawn up and many utensils have already been made. Doesn't it say somewhere in the Bible there will be a Temple in Jerusalem in the last days?"

A third man, Richard, joined the conversation. "I think you're right! And the Antichrist is supposed to establish himself as ruler in that Temple. That seems to me to be a good reason not to build it. Why make it easy for the Antichrist to have a platform from which to rule?"

Bob nodded his head in agreement. "No Temple, no Antichrist to deal with. Sounds good to me."

This conversation is not unusual. Many in today's church share the same belief, and opposition to building a Third Temple has increased. Meanwhile, many Jews in Israel are experiencing a growing desire to offer sacrifices on Temple Mount. They long for a Temple to be built where the two previous temples stood. While westerners consider a new Temple unnecessary, there is a longing for it in Israel. Why are there such opposing views on this issue? Is there a valid reason to rebuild the Temple?

As I observed growing contention surrounding this issue, I began to search the Bible for information about a third Temple. What I discovered has given me an increased desire to expose false views held by the western church. The children of God need to understand why the holy Temple should—and will—be rebuilt. As we proceed, I will present evidence that explains why and where a Third Temple will be constructed.

We begin with a quick overview of the First and Second Temples. King Solomon built the First Temple in Jerusalem around 830BC. His father, King David, had wanted to build a house in which the Lord would dwell (1 Chronicles 28), but it fell to King Solomon to oversee the actual construction (2 Chronicles 3–7). The First Temple stood more than 400 years before it was destroyed by the armies of King Nebuchadnezzar of Babylon (Jeremiah 52:12–13). When the Jews returned to Jerusalem following the Babylonian captivity, construction began on the Second Temple (Ezra 1–6). Its completion occurred about 350BC. This was the temple King Herod later expanded and built upon, completing his renovations in 37AD. Yeshua overturned the tables of the money changers in the Second Temple (Matthew 21:12–13). He also prophesied its destruction and said that not one stone would remain on another (Matthew 24:1–2). In 70AD, the Romans demolished it. There has been no attempt to rebuild it since, but that situation is about to change.

Biblical Support for a Third Temple

This is what the Lord says: "I will return to Zion and dwell in Jerusalem. Then Jerusalem will be called the

> Faithful City, and the mountain of the Lord Almighty will be called the Holy Mountain." . . . This is what the Lord Almighty says: "I will save my people from the countries of the east and the west. I will bring them back to live in Jerusalem; they will be my people, and I will be faithful and righteous to them as their God." . . . This is what the Lord Almighty says: "Just as I had determined to bring disaster on you and showed no pity when your ancestors angered me," says the Lord Almighty, "so now I have determined to do good again to Jerusalem and Judah. Do not be afraid."
> —Zechariah 8:3,7–8,14–15

These verses are eschatological (related to end-time events) and include important points. The Lord said He *will* return to Zion and He *will* dwell in Jerusalem, a definitive statement. He said the mountain of the Lord Almighty *will* be known as the Holy Mountain. Again, a definite statement. He also said He would bring His people back to Jerusalem. Today Jews are returning to Israel from all over the world.

> This is what the Lord Almighty says: "Many peoples and the inhabitants of many cities will yet come, and the inhabitants of one city will go to another and say, 'Let us go at once to entreat the Lord and seek the Lord Almighty. I myself am going.' And many peoples and powerful nations will come to Jerusalem to seek the Lord Almighty and to entreat him." This is what the Lord Almighty says: "In those days ten people from all languages and nations will take firm hold of one Jew by the hem of his robe and say, 'Let us go with you, because we have heard that God is with you.'"
> —Zechariah 8:20–23

What a remarkable statement! Gentiles "will take firm hold of [the] Jew by the hem of his robe and say, 'Let us go with you, because we have heard that God is with you.'" This sounds like the present-day Jewish Roots movement in which Christians are actively searching for biblical truth from the Jewish community.

Amazingly, an increasing number of Jews have responded and share their truth with gentiles! This interaction was unheard of until recently.

> This is what the Lord Almighty says: "You who now hear these words spoken by the prophets who were there when the foundation was laid for the house of the Lord Almighty, let your hands be strong so that the temple may be built. . ."
> —Zechariah 8:9

Bible prophecies are often applicable to two different time periods. For example, Daniel prophesied of one who would magnify himself above every god and say unheard of things against the God of gods (Daniel 11:36). He would desecrate the Temple, abolish the daily sacrifice, and set up the abomination that causes desolation (verse 31). Antiochus IV Epiphanes, the Seleucid king who reigned during the second century BC, first fulfilled this prophecy. He desecrated the Temple when he erected a statue of Zeus inside the Temple and sacrificed pigs on the altar. The same prophecy in Daniel 11 also speaks of a future fulfillment when the Antichrist will desecrate the Temple in the last days. He will establish himself above God, blaspheme Him, and make unholy sacrifices.

The prophet Malachi described an event that will take place after the construction of the Third Temple.

> "I will send my messenger, who will prepare the way before me. Then suddenly the Lord you are seeking will come to his temple; the messenger of the covenant, whom you desire, will come," says the Lord Almighty.
> —Malachi 3:1

The Lord said He will come suddenly to His temple, the Temple not in existence today. This is descriptive of His Second Coming. Every eye will see His return.

> But who can endure the day of his coming? Who can stand when he appears? For he will be like a refiner's fire or a launderer's soap. He will sit as a refiner and

CHAPTER 6: REBUILD THE TEMPLE

purifier of silver; he will purify the Levites and refine them like gold and silver. Then the Lord will have men who will bring offerings in righteousness, and the offerings of Judah and Jerusalem will be acceptable to the Lord, as in days gone by, as in former years.
—Malachi 3:2–4

This passage refutes the argument that because believers are now the temple of the Holy Spirit it is unnecessary to build a third temple. The Spirit does dwell in us, as Paul made clear in his letter to Corinth. He said, "Do you not know that your bodies are temples of the Holy Spirit, who is in you, whom you have received from God?" (1 Corinthians 6:19.) But I ask: will men bring offerings to you? Will they bring them to me? To your friend who is a believer? Of course not. God's chosen people will bring their offerings to the physical temple in Jerusalem as worship before the Lord.

Up to this point, we have seen from Zechariah and Malachi that God will suddenly return to dwell in Jerusalem on the Holy Mountain. He will come to His Temple, the House of God, on Temple Mount where men will bring offerings to the Lord as they did centuries ago.

The prophet Haggai compared the glory of the First Temple to that of the Second Temple. In the third verse of the second chapter of Haggai we read, "Who of you is left who saw this house in its former glory?" Haggai was referring to Solomon's Temple, the First Temple. Then he asked, "How does it look to you now? Does it not seem to you like nothing?" Compared to the beauty and richness of Solomon's Temple, the rebuilt Second Temple was not as beautiful. But Haggai declared in verse nine, "The glory of this present house [the Second Temple] will be greater than the glory of the former house [the First Temple], says the Lord Almighty."

If the Second Temple were not as beautiful, how could it possibly be more glorious? The reason is simple. Yeshua HaMashiach would walk in it during His time on earth. If the

179

First Temple had great glory and the Second Temple had greater glory, I believe that the Third Temple will have the greatest glory because Messiah will enter it as the Ruling King.

> "This is what the Lord Almighty says: 'In a little while I will once more shake the heavens and the earth, the sea and the dry land. I will shake all nations, and what is desired by all nations will come, and I will fill this house with glory,' says the Lord Almighty.
> —Haggai 2:6–7

The Messiah is "what is desired by all nations," and when He comes, He will shake all nations. We know this did not occur at His first coming, but it will take place when He returns.

The writer of Hebrews later quoted verse six above and further expanded it.

> See to it that you do not refuse him who speaks. If they did not escape when they refused him who warned them on earth, how much less will we, if we turn away from him who warns us from heaven? At that time his voice shook the earth, but now he has promised, "Once more I will shake not only the earth but also the heavens."
> —Hebrews 12:25–26

Not only will HaShem's voice shake the nations, His voice will also shake the heavens.

We saw earlier that when the Lord returns, He will enter His house, the Third Temple:

> ". . .'The glory of this present house will be greater than the glory of the former house,' says the Lord Almighty. 'And in this place I will grant peace,' declares the Lord Almighty."
> —Haggai 2:9

Bear with a bit of redundancy as I make my point. We just read, "'the glory of this present house will be greater than the glory of the former house,' says the Lord Almighty." While this referred to the Second Temple, it must also refer to the Third Temple because of this phrase: "'And in this place I will grant peace,' declares the Lord Almighty." Israel was not experiencing peace when Yeshua walked in the Second Temple 2,000 years ago, and there is certainly no peace for the Jewish people today. But when the Prince of Peace returns and enters "this place," which Haggai 2:9 stated will be the Third Temple, there will be peace for Israel and its people for the first time in its history.

Man did not select where God's ultimate dwelling place will be. A committee did not make the decision. God Himself made the choice when He selected Jerusalem, and that choice was set in motion when King David bought a certain threshing floor. The threshing floor was on Mount Moriah, what we know today as Temple Mount.

> So David paid Araunah six hundred shekels of gold for the site. David built an altar to the Lord there and sacrificed burnt offerings and fellowship offerings. He called on the Lord, and the Lord answered him with fire from heaven on the altar of burnt offering.
> —1 Chronicles 21:25–26

Then "David said, 'The house of the Lord God is to be here. . .'" (1 Chronicles 22:1). This is where it all started.

After King David's death, Solomon reigned over Israel and oversaw construction of the First Temple on the site of the threshing floor that his father had purchased (2 Chronicles 3:1). Solomon led a dedication ceremony when construction was complete (2 Chronicles 6–7). Solomon prayed, and the gathered throng witnessed an amazing event.

> When Solomon finished praying, fire came down from heaven and consumed the burnt offering and the sacrifices, and the glory of the Lord filled the temple. The priests could not enter the temple of the Lord because the glory of the Lord filled it.
> —2 Chronicles 7:1–2

Fire came down from heaven and consumed the burnt offering and sacrifices where the old threshing floor had been. I would love to see that event repeated in my day.

> When Solomon had finished the temple of the Lord and the royal palace... the Lord appeared to him at night and said: "I have heard your prayer and have chosen this place for myself as a temple for sacrifices..."
> —2 Chronicles 7:11–12

Read those verses one more time and note who chose where the temple would be located.

A familiar passage follows a couple of verses later.

> If my people, who are called by my name, will humble themselves and pray and seek my face and turn from their wicked ways, then I will hear from heaven, and I will forgive their sin and will heal their land. Now my eyes will be open and my ears attentive to the prayers offered in this place.
> —2 Chronicles 7:14–15

Prayer warriors quote these verses frequently when praying for our country. Reading these verses in context, however, we find they relate to the Temple, the holy place God chose to place His Name.

> I have chosen and consecrated this temple so that my Name may be there forever. My eyes and my heart will always be there.
> —2 Chronicles 7:16

Where is the heart of God? On Temple Mount. Where are His eyes? On Temple Mount. These are eternal verses. Verse 16 states once again that God chose "this place." He consecrated this Temple so His name would be there forever.

> This is what the Lord Almighty says: "I am very jealous for Zion; I am burning with jealousy for her."
> —Zechariah 8:2

In this verse God revealed His strong feelings for Jerusalem and the Holy Mountain. Because it is His chosen place, He burns with jealousy for her.

The Temple and Eschatology

This place, where God's name, heart, and eyes will be forever, is important to God. How does this holy place fit into end-time prophecy? The best source for an answer to this question is in the book of Daniel. In the ninth chapter Daniel spoke of a 70-week period. The general agreement among scholars is the first 69 weeks took place between the time of Daniel's prophesy and the day Yeshua made His triumphal entry into Jerusalem. John spoke of the 70th week in the book of Revelation, placing it in the future. Scholars consider the 70th week to be the seven-year tribulation. Mid-way through those seven years, at the 3½-year mark, the Great Tribulation will begin.

> He will confirm a covenant with many for one 'seven.' In the middle of the 'seven' he will put an end to sacrifice and offering. And on a wing of the temple he will set up an abomination that causes desolation, until the end that is decreed is poured out on him."
> —Daniel 9:27

"Many" in this verse refers to Israel. The person confirming the covenant with Israel is the Beast, also known as the Antichrist. In the middle of the seven-year period, the Beast will put an end to sacrifice and offering. These sacrifices and offerings cannot take place until the Temple is rebuilt. There is no Temple today; offerings and sacrifices are not taking place. It is interesting to note, however, that recently a group of men attempted to ascend Temple Mount with sacrificial lambs on Pesach (Passover). Their endeavor was unsuccessful. The Word of God states that a time is coming when men will present sacrifices on Mount Moriah at the Temple, and God is stirring that desire in the hearts of His people today.

Rebuilding the Temple and instituting the practice of animal sacrifice visualizes the salvation of Israel. When animal sacrifices begin, Jews worldwide will ask, "Why?" Rabbinical Judaism will not provide the answer to that question. Biblical Judaism which requires the shedding of blood for the removal of sin, will provide clarity. Yom Kippur illustrates this truth. When Israel becomes aware of this truth, Judaism will return to the Word of God. This will prepare them for Zechariah 12. They will look upon Him who was pierced, and they will know. Messiah was pierced to take away their sin, and when Israel sees that truth, they will be saved and the Kingdom of Messiah will begin.

The last half of the verse above spoke of the abomination of desolation which will take place in the Temple. A number of teachers in the church today use this verse to prove the Temple is not important. If the Beast is going to desecrate it, why build it? We know the answer to that question. God wants the Temple. He has stated it will be built, and so it will. It is His holy place forever, and to the Temple He will return.

Yeshua spoke to His disciples of this future event in Matthew 24.

> "So when you see standing in the holy place 'the abomination that causes desolation,' spoken of through the prophet Daniel. . ."
>
> —Matthew 24:15a

"When you see," Yeshua said. This *will* take place. When you see the abomination that causes desolation, the return of the Lord will be imminent. He (the Antichrist) will be standing in the holy place. We understand now what the "holy place" is and where it will be located.

Mark also wrote what Yeshua said about the signs of His return and took it one step further.

> "When you see 'the abomination that causes desolation' standing where it does not belong. . ."
> —Mark 13:14a

The reason the Beast's actions will be an abomination is because they defile the House of the Lord. The Beast has no authority to be there, yet he will make a strong attempt to take it over.

If there is any doubt about the identity of "the abomination that causes desolation," Paul provides a clear answer in 2 Thessalonians.

> Concerning the coming of our Lord Jesus Christ and our being gathered to him, we ask you, brothers and sisters, not to become easily unsettled or alarmed by the teaching allegedly from us—whether by a prophecy or by word of mouth or by letter—asserting that the day of the Lord has already come. Don't let anyone deceive you in any way, for that day will not come until the rebellion occurs and **the man of lawlessness is revealed,** the man doomed to destruction. He will oppose and will exalt himself over everything that is called God or is worshiped, so that **he sets himself up in God's temple, proclaiming himself to be God.**
> —2 Thessalonians 2:1–4 (emphasis added)

Conclusion

It is clear in God's Word that the Lord's dwelling place will be in Jerusalem. It is also clear that His dwelling place will be on Mount Moriah specifically, the location He has chosen for Himself. His house, the Temple, will be rebuilt, and it will play a critical role in the last days. When He returns to rule and reign from Jerusalem, all nations will come to the Temple on the holy mountain to worship Him.

> And they will bring all your people, from all the nations, to my holy mountain in Jerusalem as an offering to the Lord. . .
> —Isaiah 66:20a

Ask God to provide opportunities to share this information with others. Also pray that construction of His House will begin. God desires to come to His dwelling place in Jerusalem, and as believers we share in that desire.

> *Lord, we want to rebuild your house, your resting place. You have chosen Mount Zion as your habitation; you have put Your Name there. It is now and forever holy. Make a way for the Temple to be built soon. Amen.*

> Where is the house you will build for me? Where will my resting place be?
> —Isaiah 66:1

Chapter 7:

The Counterfeit

Counterfeit: to practice deception; to make a copy or imitation with the intent to deceive; to defraud; to mock. A counterfeit item is bogus. A counterfeiter is one who produces the bogus item and then passes it off as genuine, usually in a dishonest manner. Almost anything can be counterfeited: art, documents, jewelry, watches. The list is endless. Once a counterfeiter has produced an item that appears genuine, and once he masters the art of the con, his financial gain can be quite lucrative. But no matter how accomplished he is, or how much money he accumulates from his deceptive practices, there is one who is more fraudulent, more accomplished, and much more dangerous. His name is Satan, the father of lies, the one in whom no truth resides. His goal isn't money. He's after something far more valuable, the very soul of man. He utilizes every avenue of deceit at his disposal as he works without ceasing to turn God's creation away from Him. He cunningly twists the truth and sets his trap with great deliberation. Those who are not well-acquainted with the person who is Truth will fall victim to the enemy's lies and eventually accept that which is counterfeit.

The opposite of counterfeit is truth. Authentic truth can be found only in the One True God, the author of truth. He is Truth.

His Word and His Spirit reveal His truth to all mankind. To know that truth and to guard against the enemy's deception, one must know God's Word and develop an intimate relationship with the Creator. It is crucial, however, to remain alert and watchful. "Your enemy the devil prowls around like a roaring lion looking for someone to devour" (1 Peter 5:8).

Satan has meticulously employed his deceptive practices for millennia, working his way into individual lives and churches alike. He has successfully adulterated God's truth and captivated many people with his twisted form of "truth." As we proceed, we will investigate some of the counterfeit truths Satan has slyly authored. His cunning is so subtle that many believers are completely unaware of his counterfeit productions.

Nimrod

Our examination of Satan's deceptive ploys must include how he uses men to deceive others into following false beliefs. The first example begins in the land of Babylon shortly after the flood of Noah. The main character is Nimrod, Noah's great-grandson. (Noah's son Ham was the father of Cush, Nimrod's father.) Nimrod was the first king of Babylon and the first to carry out war against his neighbors. He eventually conquered all the nations from Assyria to Libya.[13] He was responsible for the construction of Nineveh, and to this day a major part of its ruins is called "Nimrod."[14] Other names by which Nimrod has been known include Kronos and Saturn, and he was the first mortal to be called a god.[15] He is called a mighty hunter in Genesis 10:8–12. He is the deified husband of the deified Semiramis and her supernatural son, Tammuz.[16] He has been called the Lord of the Mighty Ones and is sometimes depicted with

---

[13] Hislop, Rev. Alexander, *Two Babylons, or the Papal Worship Proved to be the Worship of Nimrod and His Wife* (Hunlock Creek: E World Publishing, Inc), p. 23.
[14] Hislop, p. 25.
[15] Hislop, p. 32.
[16] Hislop, p. 31.

wings. Nimrod was called "The Giant" in the Septuagint, and ancient statues of him often depict his head adorned with horns which symbolize strength.[17] Eventually, he became known as the "Father of the Gods."

Tradition from earliest times bears witness to the apostasy of Nimrod. His success at leading men away from the patriarchal faith and the awe of God is even more amazing when one considers that he accomplished this with the memory of the flood still fresh in men's minds.[18] The religion he introduced led men to believe that spiritual change was not necessary, and that regeneration was merely external. "Nimrod religion" led mankind to seek goodness in sensual enjoyment and to enjoy the pleasures of sin without fear of The Holy God.[19]

Semiramis

The second character is Nimrod's wife, Semiramis. She was deified along with her son and given the title, "Queen of Heaven."[20] She was worshiped as the incarnation of the holy spirit, and she represented the spirit of all grace that brooded over the waters of creation. She was represented by a dove and has been pictured as the dove with an olive branch in her mouth that greeted Noah.

Semiramis was known in the ancient world by many names. In Egypt her name was Athor, the Habitation of God, because people believed that all the fullness of the godhead dwelt in her. The Greeks called her Aphrodite, and she was worshiped as Venus of Rome and Astarte of Babylon, the Mother of the Gods. She was also known as Ishtar in Babylon. Under the name "Mother of the Gods,"[21] the goddess Queen of Babylon was worshiped with great veneration almost universally by the Persians

---

[17] Hislop, p. 33.
[18] Hislop, p. 52.
[19] Hislop, p. 55.
[20] Hislop, p. 75.
[21] Hislop, p. 78.

and Syrians, as well as by the kings of Europe and Asia.[22] But it wasn't only pagan nations who venerated Semiramis. Jeremiah 7:18 provides evidence that many Israelites also worshiped her.

Tammuz

The third figure is Tammuz, the son of Semiramis. He, too, was elevated to the status of "god." A more familiar name by which he became known in classical writings was Bacchus, "the lamented one."[23] Bacchus was associated with revelry, drunkenness, and orgies, the purpose of which was the purification of souls.[24] Tammuz was also known as Cupid and portrayed with the requisite wings.[25]

The Counterfeit Trinity

Nimrod, Semiramis, and Tammuz were revered as gods, and they became the perfect characters for one of Satan's devious plans. His strategy was to present this family as a false trinity. Nimrod, the "Father of all Gods," became known as the "father." Semiramis was known as the "Mother of the Gods," or "Queen of Heaven," and was depicted as a dove representing a holy spirit. Presenting Semiramis in this manner was a counterfeit of the true Holy Spirit. Semiramis was also represented by the element of air. (The Hebrew word for "air" and "spirit" is the same.)[26] Tammuz voluntarily shed his blood and died for mankind's deliverance from the wrath to come.[27] His "death and resurrection" for the purification of mankind presents him as a messiah, a counterfeit intended to replace the one true Messiah.

---

[22] Hislop, p. 80.
[23] Hislop, p. 21.
[24] Hislop, p. 22.
[25] Hislop, p. 40.
[26] Hislop, p. 79.
[27] Hislop, p. 62.

Nearly every name of the true promised Messiah was bestowed upon Tammuz. The Tenach tells us one of Messiah's names is Adonai. Similarly, Tammuz was known as Adon or Adonis. Messiah is the Mediator between God and mankind. Tammuz was worshiped as the mediator under the name Mithras. The true Lord of the Covenant is The Messiah. As Baal Berit, Tammuz was called the Lord of the Covenant. God sent His son Yeshua for the salvation of mankind. As Vishnu in India, Tammuz was called the savior of men and worshiped as the great victim-man who gave himself as a sacrifice because there was nothing else to offer.[28] In Babylon Tammuz was known as Zoroaster, "Seed of the Woman,"[29] who suffered voluntarily, crushing the serpent's head and removing sin and the curse.[30] The true "Seed of the Woman" is Yeshua and is first mentioned in Genesis 3:15. Tammuz has also been called the Branch of God.[31] Messiah is the True Branch of God (Jeremiah 23:5).

In the early ages of mankind, the existence of a sole and omnipotent deity seems to have been a universal belief.[32] The recognition of a trinity with one god in three persons was common in all ancient nations of the world. Such was the god of the Babylonians, and they symbolized this doctrine with an equilateral triangle.[33] The three persons in the counterfeit trinity became known as the eternal father, the spirit of god incarnate in a human mother, and her divine son, the fruit of that incarnation.[34] The Babylonians created images of one body with three heads to denote the trinity.[35] Buddha, whom the Japanese worship, has been depicted with three heads on his body. This commonality

---

[28] Hislop, p. 70.
[29] Hislop, p. 61.
[30] Hislop, p. 71.
[31] Hislop, p. 73.
[32] Hislop, p. 14.
[33] Hislop, p. 16.
[34] Hislop, p. 19.
[35] Hislop, p. 17.

is found in India's supreme deity, depicted with three heads on one body.

Another prominent image of Semiramis and Tammuz was that of a mother holding her infant son in her arms. After the tower of Babel was destroyed and people were scattered throughout the earth, this mother and child became known in Egypt as Isis and Osiris. In India they became known as Isi and Iswara. In Asia, Cyble and Deoris. The Romans named them Fortuna and Jupiter. The Greeks knew them as Ceres and Plutos, and in China and Japan they were known as Shing Mao and her child.[36] These allusions to the triune godhead in false religions all have their origin in the people groups present in Babylon after the flood.

God revealed Himself as the creator Father, as the Redeeming Son, and as the Holy Spirit who indwells His children. This amazing, wonderful divine truth has become known as the Holy Trinity. Long before the church utilized this phrase, however, Satan had already created a false father, son, and spirit. The perverted version that Satan established has become a strong part of all false religions, and the perversion can be found in a large portion of the church today. Largely unchallenged, it has become firmly rooted. This false trinity, which has been in existence since the days of Noah, will continue into the Babylon of end-time prophecy.

The doctrine of the true Trinity reveals that Messiah is the Creator God. He is called Eternal Father in Isaiah 9:6, and Jehovah our Righteousness in Jeremiah 23:6. Yeshua said, "I and the Father are one" (John 10:30). He also said, "If you have seen me, you have seen the Father" (John 14:9). "Before Abraham was, I Am" (John 8:58). Messiah is divine. Yeshua is God. Those who accept the Bible as the Word of God believe in this triune God (Father, Son, and Spirit) while many in the world strongly deny it. It's a difficult concept to understand. Those

---

[36] Hislop, p. 20.

who seek a logical explanation for it and find none, reject it outright. Historians have debated for years how the True Father and Son can be the same person.

Just as the true God the Father and God the Son are one, the same concept is depicted in the Babylonian counterfeit. Tammuz, the "Lamented One" adored as the child in his mother's arms, has also been called the husband of Semiramis. Nimrod, who we discussed earlier as the husband of Semiramis, has also been known as the son, Tammuz. In Egypt, Osiris (Tammuz) was represented as both the husband and the son of Isis (Semiramis), and bore the title, "Husband of the Mother." Are you confused yet? You're not alone. Those who research ancient history on this subject become confused by this "unity" as well. As the true Father, Son, and Spirit are indistinguishable, so are Nimrod the father and Tammuz the son in ancient religions. The father of lies, indeed, laid his groundwork carefully as he deviously counterfeited God's truth.

This also accounts for the confusion about Isis and Osiris. Isis is the Egyptian version of the mother, and Osiris is parallel to Tammuz. Osiris was represented as the husband and the son of his mother at the same time. He bore the title "Husband of the Mother." In India, the god Iswara is pictured as a baby at the breast of his wife Isi.[37] Nimrod and Tammuz, the son and the father, became indistinguishable from each other in ancient religions. The true Father, Son, and Spirit were perfectly counterfeited because the Father and Son of the true faith were indistinguishable. With this understanding we can now discuss the death of Nimrod, or perhaps we should say the death of the son, Tammuz.

Death of Nimrod/Tammuz

While the Bible does not mention Nimrod's death, evidence from antiquity leads to the conclusion he suffered a violent

---

[37] Hislop, p. 22.

death[38] and was mourned among all apostates. When the Egyptian women learned of his death, they wept for him. When the Phoenicians and Assyrians heard the news, they wept for Tammuz. In turn, the Greeks and Romans wept for Bacchus, the Lamented One.[39] Even the women of Israel mourned the death of the counterfeit deity (Ezekiel 8:14). After Nimrod died, he was deified and granted yet another name, Orion, and given a place among the stars.

God's Warning

Shortly after the flood, God chose a man named Abraham and initiated with him the Abrahamic Covenant. Years later, after God led His people out of Egypt and brought them to Mount Sinai, He warned them to never participate in any form of pagan worship. Their worship was to be reserved for the Lord, who was a jealous God. He gave this warning because the counterfeit trinity was already firmly embedded in all pagan religions.

> Do not worship any other god, for the Lord, whose name is Jealous, is a jealous God. Be careful not to make a treaty with those who live in the land; for when they prostitute themselves to their gods and sacrifice to them, they will invite you and you will eat their sacrifices.
> —Exodus 34:14–15

In addition, God gave His people strict instructions concerning the objects of pagan worship. Upon taking possession of the land the Lord would give to them, they were to:

> Destroy completely all the places on the high mountains, on the hills and under every spreading tree, where the nations you are dispossessing worship their gods. Break down their altars, smash their sacred stones and burn their Asherah poles in the fire; cut down the idols of their

---

[38] Hislop, p. 57.
[39] Hislop, p. 56.

gods and wipe out their names from those places. **You must not worship the Lord your God in their way.**
—Deuteronomy 12:2–4 (emphasis added)

In verses 5, 11, and 14 of this chapter God specified the place where His people were to worship. It would be a place He would choose:

> Be careful not to sacrifice your burnt offerings anywhere you please. Offer them only at the place the Lord will choose in one of your tribes, and there observe everything I command you.
> —Deuteronomy 12:13–14

Similar commands, laws, and warnings are numerous in the Tenach. The Holy Lord did not want His people involved in anything related to false gods. Even the names of the false gods were to be wiped out. Why? He is a jealous God. He alone was to be worshiped. He warned His people numerous times of the consequences if they disobeyed. They would lose the blessings of God, and they would be conquered and carried away to other lands. The Tenach records that the people of God stumbled and disobeyed God's commands on many occasions. They wandered far from God and suffered the consequences. Then they would repent and turn back to God. The history of Israel reflects a continuing cycle of blessing, sin, judgment, and repentance.

Israel's rebellion ultimately led to the departure of God's glory from Solomon's Temple. Two specific things were instrumental in His presence being withdrawn. First, the women of Israel had mourned the death of Tammuz at the Temple (Ezekiel 8:14). This deified son from Babylon, the counterfeit Messiah, was being worshiped in God's holy place. Against God's clear instructions, the holy and the counterfeit had been mixed together.

The book of Jeremiah provides insight into the second reason God's glory departed from the Temple:

> The children gather wood, the fathers light the fire, and the women knead the dough and make cakes to offer to the Queen of Heaven.
> —Jeremiah 7:18a

The Israelites were worshiping Semiramis, the deified wife of Nimrod, the mother of Tammuz. Their actions brought a strong response from God:

> 'Therefore this is what the Sovereign Lord says: "My anger and my wrath will be poured out on this place... Therefore say to them, 'This is the nation that has not obeyed the Lord its God or responded to correction. Truth has perished; it has vanished from their lips.'"
> —Jeremiah 7:20a, 28

God's truth was absent. The counterfeit had infiltrated Israel to the point that truth was dead. Once truth is destroyed, holiness is as well. God's people had disobeyed Him by mixing the holy with the profane. When truth contains even a hint of falsehood, it is no longer truth. The Israelites found it difficult to keep God's holy place pure and undefiled. God is a holy God with a desire for His people to be holy. Strong's definition of the Hebrew word for holy, *kadosh*, is "separate," that which is pure. When something is sanctified (the same Hebrew word as holy), it is set apart and considered holy. It is consecrated to the holy God and set aside for worship. Conversely, adding anything counterfeit to that which is holy renders it unholy, unclean, no longer pure.

Another situation arose where the unholy was permitted to enter the Tabernacle. The tenth chapter of Leviticus relates what happened when members of the priesthood decided they had a better way to worship the Lord:

> Aaron's sons Nadab and Abihu took their censers, put fire in them and added incense; and they offered unauthorized fire before the Lord, contrary to his command. So fire came out from the presence of the Lord and consumed them, and they died before the Lord. Moses then said to Aaron, "This is what the Lord spoke of when he said: 'Among those who approach me I will be proved holy; in the sight of all the people I will be honored.'" Aaron remained silent.
> —Leviticus 10:1–3

God had given the Israelites specific instructions regarding the fire in the tabernacle. The priests were to take fire from the brazen altar to light the coals on the altar of incense. This was holy fire. Nadab and Abihu obtained their fire from a different source, making it unauthorized and unholy. Swiftly, God responded to Nadab's and Abihu's unholy act. One of the functions of the priesthood was to instruct the Israelites how to discern the difference between that which was holy and that which was not. In this case, the priests failed in their duty and God intervened.

> They are to teach my people the difference between the holy and the common and show them how to distinguish between the unclean and the clean.
> —Ezekiel 44:23

Since God is holy and wanted His people to regard Him as holy, He gave many commands in His Word regarding how He was to be worshiped. What follows is a very small sample of His instructions.

> Ascribe to the Lord the glory due his name; bring an offering and come before him. Worship the Lord in the splendor of his holiness.
> —1 Chronicles 16:29

> God is spirit, and his worshipers must worship in the Spirit and in truth.
> —John 4:24

The Bible states numerous times that the Lord God is Holy, pure, and clean. He is set apart, separate, mixed with nothing. In the book of Revelation, the Lord God spoke as the one "who is holy and true." God alone is worthy of worship and we are to honor His wishes as we worship Him. We should remove that which is unholy from our lives and seek to worship a pure and holy God in a pure and holy manner. That alone is wholly acceptable to Him.

A Brief Look into Church History

The New Covenant Church began in Jerusalem on Shavuot (Pentecost). Jews from Israel and many other countries had gathered in Jerusalem to celebrate Shavuot, the Feast of Weeks, one of three pilgrimage holidays. Many had traveled a long distance to attend this holy event. It was there, two thousand years ago, that the Holy Spirit was poured out and the church was born. The Jews gathered at the Temple heard, each in their own language, of the wonders of God (Acts 2:11). Then Peter stood up and addressed the crowd. He preached a powerful message that resulted in the baptism of 3,000 people (Acts 2:14–41).

Initially, the church was made up entirely of Jews, but it wasn't long before gentiles began to experience the saving grace of Yeshua. While this was part of God's master plan (see Ephesians 2 and Romans 11), it caused a great deal of consternation among the Jews. Gentiles were considered unclean and were to be avoided. Many Jews believed if gentiles were to become part of the church, then they should convert to Judaism and be circumcised. Other Jews disagreed, and a big debate ensued. After a great deal of discussion, the decision was made to allow gentiles into the church without becoming a proselytized Jew (Acts 15).

The church remained Jewish in its practices until the time of Constantine, the Roman Emperor who ruled from 306–337AD. His influence dramatically changed the direction of the church at the Council of Nicea in 325AD. This Council was astonishingly anti-Semitic, and it ultimately outlawed the Jewish-ness of the original church. Many anti-biblical changes were instituted, including changing the day of Shabbat (the Sabbath) from Saturday to Sunday, removing the Feasts of the Lord from the church, and incorporating pagan practices into church rituals and holidays.

From this point forward, it would be the sword of the empire, rather than the sword of the Spirit, that would rule the church.[40] The empire's Greco-Roman culture was such a strong influence that the church began to incorporate many of its unbiblical tenets. Eventually, this led the church into Catholicism and later into the Dark Ages. As anti-Semitism and paganism spread in the church, an unscriptural Christianity emerged that continues today. The church has become so entangled in centuries of tradition that most members, including many church leaders, are unaware of where Biblical teaching ends and pagan practices begin.

The Two Major Christian Holidays

As Rome became Christianized by Constantine, and as all things Jewish were being stripped from the church, a plan was developed to make it easy for pagan Romans to accept Christianity. The plan was to incorporate pagan rituals into newly created Christian holidays. One of the major pagan celebrations the church assimilated was associated with the winter solstice, the day with the shortest amount of daylight. This day, and the days that followed, were of great importance to the Romans and the Babylonians before them because they worshiped the sun. Unbelievers were more inclined to join the church when they could worship God with a familiar pagan element.

---

[40] Gerrish, Jim, *Does God Play Favorites: Exploring God's Plan for Israel* (Katy: Cornerstone Publishing, 2000), p. 170.

We discussed earlier that the Babylonians believed Tammuz died for the sins of the world. They believed his death occurred on the winter solstice. Three days after he died, the sun began to rise higher in the sky and appear to come closer to the earth. Tammuz' resurrection from the dead was celebrated on this day. As Nimrod and Tammuz were worshiped as the one true god, the sun god, this became a celebration of the death and rebirth of the unconquered sun.

There are many examples of pagan worship during the winter solstice. In addition to celebrating Tammuz' resurrection on the third day after the winter solstice, his birthday was observed on the same day. This birthday of the counterfeit son of god was observed far and wide in all realms of paganism, and by some in the church. Not only did it commemorate the birthday of Tammuz the Great Deliverer, but the birth of the sun.[41] The ancient Egyptians believed the son of Isis, Osiris (the Egyptian name for Tammuz), was born at this very time.[42] In ancient Rome, the Feast of Saturn was celebrated on the winter solstice with considerable festivity and drunkenness. When Rome became Christianized by Constantine, Yeshua was simply substituted for Saturn. Another name for this holiday was Yule Day. ("Yule" was the Chaldean word for "infant.")

These pagan beliefs and rituals became a perfect foundation for Constantine to institute a major holiday to celebrate Yeshua's birth. It would be the perfect Satan-inspired counterfeit. Just as pagans celebrated the virgin birth of Tammuz, the counterfeit son of god, the church would officially celebrate—on the same day—the virgin birth of Yeshua HaMashiach, Son of the Living God. Since the Bible does not provide the date of Yeshua's birth,[43] it became convenient for Constantine to declare December 25th as His birthday. The church holiday became known as Christmas, or Christmastide.

---

[41] Hislop, p. 94.
[42] Hislop, p. 93.
[43] Hislop, p. 93.

CHAPTER 7: THE COUNTERFEIT

Two symbols long associated with Christmas, the Yule Log and the Christmas tree, have their roots in paganism as well. The Christmas tree was common in pagan Rome, Egypt, and Greece long before the coming of Messiah. The mother of the sun god Adonis was said to have been changed into a tree, and it was in that form she gave birth to a divine son. This led to the Christmas Eve tradition of placing a dead Yule log on the fire. The following morning a live tree would "appear." These became known as the Branch of God and the tree that brings all divine gifts to men.[44] It symbolized the newborn lord of the covenant who, after his death, had risen triumphant over his enemies.

Another pagan ritual associated with burning a dead log on the winter solstice was in commemoration of Tammuz' death. Three days after it was burned a live tree was decorated to celebrate his resurrection. Others believed the Yule Log represented the dead stock of Nimrod, the sun god who had been killed by his enemies. On the third day after it was burned, a tree was decorated to represent Nimrod's resurrection. Babylonian paganism corrupted truth to the point that an evil counterfeit has made its way to the ends of the earth.[45]

Pagans held a celebration in the spring that was associated with Semiramis of Babylon, the Queen of Heaven, deified mother of Tammuz and wife of Nimrod. Semiramis established a holy day to commemorate the death and resurrection of Tammuz, as well as a 40-day period of weeping leading up to the anniversary of Tammuz' death. This mandate included an edict that meat could not be consumed during the mourning period. The celebration of the death and resurrection of the counterfeit son in the counterfeit trinity was brought into the church and made "Christian" by commemorating the death and resurrection of the true Son of God on the same day. The 40-day period of mourning for Tammuz was kept by the church and given a new name,

---

[44] Hislop, p. 98.
[45] Hislop, p. 98.

Lent. This newly created holiday was called Easter, named after Ishtar, one of Semiramis' many names.

After Nimrod died, Semiramis claimed he really wasn't deceased, but had ascended into heaven where he became the sun god. This appears to be a bit self-serving of Semiramis as her declaration automatically made her a goddess, the wife of a god. To give validation to her title, she supposedly ascended into heaven after she died and then returned to earth in a giant egg that landed on the banks of the Euphrates River. When the egg opened, Astarte [Semiramis], the goddess of love, emerged.[46] This virgin goddess was supernaturally impregnated by a sunbeam [a representation of the Holy Spirit] from the sun god Nimrod [a representation of God the Father], and later gave birth to the sun god Tammuz [a representation of God the Son].[47] Recall that Nimrod and Tammuz were considered one god. Early pagans believed this represented the beginning of spring as new life sprang forth, and Semiramis became known as the goddess of spring and fertility. Eggs became associated with fertility, and the Roman church adopted this mystic egg of Astarte/Ishtar and consecrated it as a symbol of Messiah's resurrection.[48]

Like the Easter egg, the Easter Bunny originated from the worship of Astarte/Ishtar. Rabbits have long been known for their prolific reproductive abilities and, as Astarte/Ishtar was the goddess of fertility, rabbits became her earthly symbol.

Before Constantine incorporated the counterfeit into Christian worship, the early church celebrated the Feast of Pesach, or Passover, each spring. Symbolically, this Feast represented the death, burial, and resurrection of Messiah, and it had been celebrated by Jews for centuries. When Constantine and the Council of Nicea removed Jewish practices from the church, Pesach was replaced with Easter, complete with its pagan origins.

---

[46] Hislop, p. 109.
[47] Hislop, p. 305.
[48] Hislop, p. 110.

CHAPTER 7: THE COUNTERFEIT

The pagan beliefs and practices we have discussed here were in existence 2,000 years before the arrival of the true Messiah. They were spread throughout the world and are still in existence today. After being officially incorporated into church doctrine at the Council of Nicea, they have become so deeply entrenched in church tradition that removing them seems impossible.

It's worth noting that pagans were deliberate in not mixing Christianity into their religions. Unfortunately, we have seen that the church was not as intentional. Even before Constantine began introducing pagan elements into the church, some Christians were already taking part in pagan rituals. As un-Godly practices became more prevalent, God-honoring men took a stand against the evil seeping into the church. One early Christian author, Tertullian (c. 150–222AD), lamented the paganization of the Roman church. He wrote that heathens were more faithful to their paganism than the church was to their holy God. Despite objections raised by Tertullian and other upright men, apostasy continued.

A Further Look into Church History

In 70AD, the Romans, under the rule of Titus, destroyed Jerusalem and the Temple. Beginning in the first century and continuing for two hundred years, Christians who refused to follow Roman-prescribed pagan worship were persecuted for their faith. About one hundred years later, Origen (c. 185–c. 254) began teaching the allegorical hermeneutic (interpretation and application) of the Word that ultimately led to replacement theology. The main tenets of this doctrine held that God was finished with Israel and the church had taken Israel's place as God's chosen people. This belief gained acceptance as Jewish practices were banned from the church. In the Fourth Century, Roman Emperor Constantine assumed power. During his reign, he issued an edict that protected Christians and made Christianity lawful in the Roman Empire. The Roman church remained anti-Semitic, however, and all Jewish roots of the church continued to be severed.

Even though Constantine declared Christianity lawful, he and his family still worshiped the sun. He called the Unconquered Sun "my companion." In 321 AD, he legislated that the venerable day of the sun (Sunday) would replace the Jewish Sabbath in honor of the sun.[49] In addition, the date of Resurrection Sunday was changed so it would not coincide with the Feast of First Fruits on the Jewish calendar.

As discussed earlier, Christmas and Easter celebrations have their roots in pagan worship. Over the course of 2,000 years, however, those origins have been mostly forgotten. The passage of time has allowed the church to become accustomed to the mixture of Christianity and paganism, and to accept as tradition the rites associated with the holidays. As stated earlier, most church members are ignorant of the origin and history of Christmas and Easter. There is no reason to question something that has "always been there." Many who are aware of the truth believe it is acceptable to take part in what has become church tradition. They maintain it is perfectly acceptable to celebrate these unbiblical holidays because they are worshiping God. They presume that God is okay with that position. Additional insight on this matter has been provided by Yeshua in the book of Revelation.

> To the angel of the church in Pergamum write: These are the words of him who has the sharp, double-edged sword. I know where you live—where Satan has his throne. Yet you remain true to my name. You did not renounce your faith in me, not even in the days of Antipas, my faithful witness, who was put to death in your city—where Satan lives. Nevertheless, I have a few things against you: There are some among you who hold to the teaching of Balaam, who taught Balak to entice the Israelites to sin so that they ate food sacrificed to idols and committed

---

[49]C. J. Koster, *Come Out of Her, My People* (South Africa: Institute for Scripture Research, 1986), p. 13.

sexual immorality. Likewise, you also have those who hold to the teaching of the Nicolaitans. Repent therefore! Otherwise, I will soon come to you and will fight against them with the sword of my mouth. Whoever has ears, let them hear what the Spirit says to the churches. To the one who is victorious, I will give some of the hidden manna. I will also give that person a white stone with a new name written on it, known only to the one who receives it.

—Revelation 2:12–17

While the letter to Pergamum represents the age of Constantine prophetically, the application of the letter applies to the church throughout history. It is as important and applicable today as it was when John wrote it. The church at Pergamum was commended for staying true to God's name and not denying their faith, even when Antipas was put to death for standing on his faith. Because Antipas refused to integrate his paganism with his faith, he was martyred. Antipas' name means "against all," a worthy name as he was against all mixture.

To understand the phrase, "I know where you live—where Satan has his throne," we need to understand Pergamum's place in history. After Cyrus conquered Babylon in 539BC, the pagan priesthood was moved to Pergamum, where they established their central college. Thus, the city which was one of the major cultural centers of the Greek world became the center of all paganism—the seat of Satan's throne. Later, when Attalus III left his kingdom to Rome in 133BC, Pergamum became part of the Roman Empire.[50]

After commending the church in Pergamum, Yeshua said he had a few things against it. His first concern was about those who held "to the teaching of Balaam." Balaam was a prophet hired by Balak, king of Moab, to curse Israel. Every time Balaam opened his mouth to curse Israel, God caused Balaam to speak words of blessing instead. Having failed in the cursing department,

---

[50] Koster, p. 92.

he decided to change tactics. Balaam told Balak to instruct the Moabites and Midianites to have their women seduce the men of Israel. That should bring about Israel's downfall, he told Balak. The Moabites and Midianites heeded Balaam's advice, set the trap, and the men of Israel fell into it. It wasn't long before the foreign women invited the Israelites to sacrifice to their pagan gods. The men eventually bowed down before the false gods in worship. God had previously warned Israel not to "seek a treaty of friendship with them [Ammonite or Moabite] as long as you live" (See Deuteronomy 23:6). Israel's disobedience caused the Lord's wrath to burn against them. Israel was cursed and many died in a subsequent plague. Even though the downfall of Israel didn't come about in the way Balak had initially planned, his goal had been realized. (See Numbers 22–24; Revelation 2:14.)

The real problem in Pergamum's church was intermarriage with the pagan world, and the Lord called that mixture the "teaching of Balaam." The name "Pergamum" means "mixed marriage."[51] Some in the assembly had encouraged the mixture of the holy with the profane. They believed it was acceptable and that God was fine with it. But the lesson we learn from Balaam's story is that the encouragement of corruption by intermarriage results in fornication and idolatry. Clearly, God does not accept such a mixture. In His letter to Pergamum, the Lord said, "Repent therefore! Otherwise, I will soon come to you and will fight against them with the sword of my mouth" (see Revelation 2:16).

There is a distinction. On one side there is Antipas "my faithful witness," and on the other Balaam's mixture. These contrasting views can be seen throughout church history and to some extent continue today. At the time of Constantine, the church became married to the state. As Christianity became the religion of Rome, the general population was persuaded to be

---

[51] Missler, Chuck, *Revelation* audio series, Supplemental Notes, p. 32.

baptized into the church without any regard to their personal faith. The Romans already worshiped many gods, and they viewed their change as simply adding this new Christian God to their collection. They brought their pagan practices into the church, and the eventual result was spiritual fornication and idolatry. This planted the seeds for what would later become the Roman Catholic Church. Thus, the church was rightly condemned for holding to the teaching of Balaam.[52] Apologist William Schnoebelen succinctly stated that since the church could not be persecuted out of existence, Satan worked to plant his throne within the church and defile it out of existence. He nearly succeeded. If you can't beat them, join them.[53]

High Places

God commanded the Israelites numerous times to destroy the places where previous occupants of the land had worshiped their false gods. They were also instructed not to worship in the same manner the nations worshiped their false gods. They were certainly not to worship the one true God in the "high places." God alone would choose where the Israelites were to worship Him (Deuteronomy 12:3–7). History shows, however, that Israel didn't always do well when it came to obeying God's commands. Accounts in 1 Kings and 2 Kings describe how Israel's kings, both good and bad, dealt with the high places.

We look first at Solomon, one of Israel's most famous kings.

> The people, however, were still sacrificing at the high places, because a temple had not yet been built for the Name of the Lord. Solomon showed his love for the Lord by walking according to the instructions given him by his father David, except that he offered sacrifices and burned incense on the high places. The king went to Gibeon to offer sacrifices, for that was the most important

---
[52] Fruchtenbaum, Arnold, *Footsteps of the Messiah* (San Antonio: Ariel Ministries, 2003), p. 43.
[53] Schnoebelen, William, *Straight Talk on the Seven Churches of Revelation*, p. 5.

high place, and Solomon offered a thousand burnt offerings on that altar.

—1 Kings 3:2–4

Two things were happening in this situation. First, the tabernacle had been placed on the high place at Gibeon. Second, Israel was worshiping God there. Both circumstances were in direct violation of God's commands. It's interesting to note what happened after Solomon made his abundant offerings. "The Lord appeared to Solomon in a dream by night: and God said, 'Ask what I shall give thee.'" Included in Solomon's reply were these words: "So give your servant a discerning heart to govern your people and to distinguish between right and wrong." This humble request pleased the Lord and He responded by giving Solomon a wise and discerning heart. After his encounter with the Lord, Solomon discontinued offering sacrifices on the high place in Gibeon. He returned to Jerusalem, God's chosen place of worship, and there offered sacrifices before the Ark of the Covenant (see 1 Kings 3).

There were other good kings. Asa, King of Judah, "did what was right in the eyes of the Lord. . . Although he did not remove the high places, Asa's heart was fully committed to the Lord all his life." (1 Kings 15:11, 14). Jehoshaphat, King of Judah, "in everything. . . followed the ways of his father Asa and did not stray from them; he did what was right in the eyes of the Lord. The high places, however, were not removed, and the people continued to offer sacrifices and burn incense there." (See 1 Kings 22:43.) Joash, King of Judah, "did what was right in the eyes of the Lord all the years Jehoiada the priest instructed him. The high places, however, were not removed; the people continued to offer sacrifices and burn incense there. (See 2 Kings 12:2–3.) Likewise, Amaziah, King of Judah, "did what was right in the eyes of the Lord. . . The high places, however, were not removed; the people continued to offer sacrifices and burn incense there." (See 2 Kings 14:3–4.) Azariah, King of Judah, "did what was right in the eyes of the Lord, just as his father Amaziah had done. The high places, however, were not removed; the people continued to offer sacrifices and burn incense there." (See 2 Kings 15:3–4.)

All these men were good kings. They followed the Lord and loved Him with all their heart. They continued to worship YHVH and never turned from Him to indulge in Baal worship. But the most important thing was missing: the high places were not removed. They remained a constant temptation to the Israelites. God made it clear *He would not allow mixed worship* when He commanded Israel not to worship Him as the nations had worshiped their gods. (See Deuteronomy 12.) Instead of heeding His words, Israel went to the high places and worshiped their Holy God in a pagan setting and context. They paid allegiance to the profane as well as the holy. Alfred Edersheim described this as a form of "Jehovah worship on the heights."[54] On the surface, it appeared to be acceptable because God was being worshiped. As a result of this attitude, mixing the profane with the holy became accepted as tradition.[55]

Many similarities can be found when comparing how Israel handled the high places and how today's church handles its "high places." Israel was unwilling to tear down the pagan high places, allowing their traditions to replace God's acceptable methods of worship. Today, the church continues to allow pagan beliefs and biblical truths to be mixed, thus creating its own "high place." The result is that many followers of Yeshua worship God within a counterfeit context. Tradition has rendered this acceptable. Two obvious examples are the two holidays previously discussed, Christmas and Easter. Both are kept within a framework that was originally pagan. Tradition has been well established, and the customs of both holidays seem to be set in concrete. That isn't to say the church doesn't love the Lord. But because

---

[54] Edersheim, Alfred, *Bible History of the Old Testament* (Peabody: Hendrickson Publishers, Inc., 1995), p. 192.
[55] Halley, Henry H., *Halley's Bible Handbook* (Grand Rapids: Zondervan Publishing Company), p. 98.

of ignorance, apathy, or believing all is well because God is still being worshiped, the "high places" remain. The history of ancient Israel parallels the history of the church in this regard.

There is good news. Israel had two kings who *did* tear down the high places. The first was King Hezekiah of Judah:

> He did what was right in the eyes of the Lord, just as his father David had done. He removed the high places, smashed the sacred stones and cut down the Asherah poles. He broke into pieces the bronze snake Moses had made, for up to that time the Israelites had been burning incense to it. (It was called Nehushtan.)
> —2 Kings 18:3–4

The second was King Josiah of Judah:

> Just as he had done at Bethel, Josiah removed all the shrines at the high places that the kings of Israel had built in the towns of Samaria and that had aroused the Lord's anger.
> —2 Kings 23:19

These kings went all the way by not allowing *any* mixture of the holy with the profane. In these last days my prayer is that God will raise up Hezekiahs and Josiahs to stand for true holiness, whatever the cost.

Jewish Roots

This brings us to the New Covenant congregation and the Jewish roots of the church. We will begin with God's instructions for His people to observe the Feasts of the Lord at specific appointed times. There were seven feasts, the first four celebrated in the Spring, the remaining three in the Fall.

The first of these annual feasts was Passover. On this day each Jewish family was required to present the sacrifice of a spotless, unblemished lamb at the Temple. This served as a prophetic picture of Yeshua, the spotless (sinless) Lamb of God who sacrificed His life to save the world from their sin. Israelites were also required to eat only bread prepared without leaven (matzah), which represented the sinlessness of Yeshua. This unleavened bread had stripes and was pierced with small holes, representing the wounds Yeshua would suffer before and during His crucifixion. His death occurred on Passover, and in every way, He fulfilled the first Feast.

The Feast of Unleavened Bread was the day after Passover. During the Passover Seder, three pieces of matzah were placed in a bag. One piece was removed and broken in half, representing Yeshua's broken body. The broken piece was then wrapped in a cloth (afikomen) and hidden somewhere in the house. Later in the Seder, children would search for the afikomen. The child who found it returned it to the father who paid a redemption price to the child. Yeshua is the Unleavened Bread, spotless and sinless. He was in the grave on the Feast of Unleavened Bread, fulling the second Feast.

The Feast of First Fruits took place the day after the Feast of Unleavened Bread. This marked the beginning of the barley harvest. On this day a sheaf of barley was presented as a wave offering before the Lord. It was only after the wave offering that the rest of the grain could be harvested. Yeshua rose from the dead on the Feast of First Fruits. He fulfilled this feast by being the first fruits of those who had died, the First Fruits of the resurrection (see 1 Corinthians 15:20–23). The first three feasts, taking place over three days, represent Yeshua's death, burial, and resurrection. Yeshua fulfilled each one on the day of the appropriate feast.

The fourth feast was the Feast of Weeks, or Shavuot. This feast had a special offering that involved waving two loaves of bread before the Lord. God required one loaf to be unleavened and one to be made with leaven. This was a picture of the "one new man" that is made up of both Jew and Gentile. In his letter to the Ephesians, Paul explained that Yeshua made these two groups one by destroying the barrier between them through His shed blood (Ephesians 2). This feast was fulfilled when Yeshua sent the Holy Spirit on Shavuot. His Spirit was poured out and became available to both Jew and Gentile.

The remaining three feasts have yet to be fulfilled. The fifth feast is the Feast of Trumpets, a picture of the rapture of the saints. The sixth is Yom Kippur which represents the salvation of Israel, as well as Yeshua's physical return to earth. The seventh and last feast is the Feast of Tabernacles, representing the thousand-year reign of Messiah from Jerusalem. These three feasts occur in the fall and will be fulfilled by the ruling King Messiah at His second coming.

One New Man

Originally, the New Covenant congregation of the Lord Yeshua was made up of Jews and proselytes to Judaism. The first recorded gentiles to enter the church were Cornelius and his friends and family (Acts 10). Cornelius was a Roman centurion who lived in Caesarea. He and his family had forsaken the pagan gods of Rome and had begun to worship the God of Israel. Peter went to Cornelius' house and spoke about God to the large group who had gathered there. The Holy Spirit came upon all who heard Peter's message and they began to speak in tongues and praise God. Upon seeing this, Peter said, "Surely no one can stand in the way of their being baptized with water. They have received the Holy Spirit just as we have." He ordered that they be baptized in the name of Yeshua (Acts 10:47–48). More gentiles followed and were accepted into the church that remained entirely Jewish in its practices.

As mentioned previously, Paul addressed how the Jew and Gentile together became "one new man" in his letter to the Ephesians (chapter 2). The eleventh chapter of his letter to Romans reiterates this concept using a biblical context of the New Covenant Church. Paul explained that gentiles by birth were separate from

Messiah and excluded from Israel because they were foreigners to the covenants of Israel. They were without hope and without God. But God had a plan through which gentiles would be included in the covenants through the shed blood of Yeshua. The shedding of blood by the Messiah of Israel made a way for gentiles to become fellow citizens with Israel.

It is important to note that since the time of Noah, God only made covenants with the nation of Israel. The Abrahamic, Davidic, and New Covenants were all made with Israel. When Paul wrote his letter to the Romans, he told them they were wild olive branches that the Lord had grafted into the olive tree of Israel (Romans 11:17), making it possible for them to enjoy the blessings of the New Covenant. Any gentile who chose to believe that Yeshua had shed his blood for the forgiveness of their sins would be grafted into Israel's covenant. The New Covenant church is Israeli.

God frequently used "pictures" in His Word to reveal His plans and purposes. One such picture is found in the story of Ruth the Moabite. There are many layers to this story, but our focus will be on one aspect, or picture. The story begins when a Jewish family moved away from Bethlehem due to a severe famine. Elimelek, Naomi, and their two sons traveled to Moab and settled there. Eventually, the sons married Moabite women. At some point Naomi's husband and sons died, which left the three women alone with no one to provide for them. This presented an extremely dire situation for the women as they had no one to provide for them. When Naomi heard that the famine was over in Bethlehem, she prepared to return to her homeland. To avoid becoming a burden to her daughters-in-law, she advised them to go back to their families and make new lives for themselves.

One daughter-in-law, Orpah, quickly made the decision to do just that. The other daughter-in-law, Ruth, begged to accompany Naomi.

> "Don't urge me to leave you or to turn back from you. Where you go I will go, and where you stay I will stay. Your people will be my people and your God my God. Where you die I will die, and there I will be buried. May the Lord deal with me, be it ever so severely, if even death separates you and me."
> —Ruth 1:16–17

Naomi eventually relented and allowed Ruth to accompany her back to Bethlehem. There, Ruth eventually married an Israelite named Boaz, a kinsman-redeemer, a type of Yeshua. Ruth, a gentile, attached herself to Israel, loved Israel, was accepted into Israel, and became an Israelite. Ruth and Boaz's union stretches into eternity. One of their sons was Obed, the father of Jesse, who was the father of David. Ruth is in the lineage of Yeshua HaMashiach (Matthew 1:5). God provided a beautiful picture of how gentiles can be grafted into Israel in the context of Israel's covenant, just as Paul would much later explain in his letters to the Romans and Ephesians.

Reformation

We read in Acts that as more gentiles accepted Yeshua's saving work on the cross and received the Holy Spirit, believing Jews found themselves in a quandary. "What do we do with all the gentiles in the church?" This question prompted a huge debate. After much deliberation, Jewish leaders decided it was acceptable to allow gentiles into the church just as they were. (See Acts 15.) Ironically, a similar question was asked at the Council of Nicea 300 years later. "What do we do with all the Jews in the church?" This time the discussion ended on a very different note. The Jews were out, and all things Jewish were eliminated from the church. Since then, the Romanized church, or one could call it the Hellenized, Westernized, or paganized church, has been out of biblical context. During the Dark Ages literacy outside the church was rare, making it easy for the church to control what people heard and learned about God. None of

CHAPTER 7: THE COUNTERFEIT

its teachings included the Jewish roots of their faith. Instead, the Jewish foundation of their faith was completely ignored and eventually forgotten.

Just as Israel went into the Diaspora in 70AD and moved away from its biblical roots (the Holy Land), the church went into its own diaspora when it was cut off from its Biblical roots (Israel). Throughout history there have been glimpses of hope. One such glimpse occurred during the Protestant Reformation. Martin Luther became one of the catalysts for the Reformation when he refused to align himself with many of the church's doctrines. While this eventually led to his excommunication, his proclamations brought many changes. Another glimpse of hope occurred when the Jews began to return to Israel in the twentieth century. At the same time, the "Christian" church began turning back to its biblical Jewish roots. Biblical Zionism, once unknown within the church, is becoming more mainstream. At the same time, replacement theology is on its way out. The practice of blessing Israel is taught in more and more churches. Reformation is advancing, and people are turning back to the Bible and the biblical context of the church.

Progress has been made, but changes are still needed. Today's church remains predominantly reformed Catholicism. Rome's two mixed holidays, Christmas and Easter, are still observed. Attempts were made during the Protestant Reformation to remove these pagan celebrations from the church, but those endeavors failed. In the sixteenth century, English Protestants attacked the pagan use of Christmas trees and mistletoe. Oliver Cromwell condemned the holiday. From 1642 to 1652 England passed laws that forbade all Christmas church services. The early Puritans brought these views with them to America, and in 1659 they passed a law forbidding Christmas in their towns.[56] Tradition won out, however, and these changes were not long-lasting.

---

[56] *Merit Students Encyclopedia,* Vol. 5, (Macmillan Educational Corporation), p. 478.

Just as Israel placed their traditions ahead of the Word, the church has placed their beloved traditions ahead of the Word. The church has chosen to ignore the Word's prohibition of these mixtures. Church leaders were to teach the difference between the holy and the profane. They were to lead people to worship our holy God in a holy manner. Sadly, this hasn't happened.

Reformation must continue. The Messianic Kingdom is coming soon, and it will be a Jewish kingdom ruled by the Jewish Messiah, the Messiah who comes from the Jewish city of Jerusalem in the Jewish nation of Israel. The counterfeit will have no place in the Messianic Kingdom. Rather, His kingdom will be *holy and pure.*

May the Holy One of Israel sanctify His people. Amen.

Note: Repeating this material must be done in a spirit of love, compassion, and humility by the leading of the Holy Spirit only.
—Pastor Marty Gale

www.ingramcontent.com/pod-product-compliance
Lightning Source LLC
LaVergne TN
LVHW051518070426
835507LV00023B/3168